John Churton Collins, Cyril Tourneur

Plays and Poems

In Two Volumes. Vol. II

John Churton Collins, Cyril Tourneur

Plays and Poems
In Two Volumes. Vol. II

ISBN/EAN: 9783744709217

Printed in Europe, USA, Canada, Australia, Japan

Cover: Foto ©Thomas Meinert / pixelio.de

More available books at **www.hansebooks.com**

THE
PLAYS AND POEMS
OF
CYRIL TOURNEUR

EDITED

With Critical Introduction and Notes

BY JOHN CHURTON COLLINS

IN TWO VOLUMES.—VOL. II.

London
CHATTO AND WINDUS, PICCADILLY
1878

THE
REVENGERS
TRAGÆDIE

As it hath been sundry times acted by the
Kings Maiestie's Seruants

AT LONDON
Printed by *G. Eld*, and are to be soul at his house
in Fleet-lane, at the signe of the
Printers-Presse
1608

Dramatis Personæ

The old Duke	
Lussurioso	*his son*
Spurio	*his bastard son*
Ambitioso	*Brothers to Lussurioso*
Supervacuo	
Vindici	*the Revenger*
Hippolito	*his brother*
Antonio	*an aged lord*
The Duchess' younger son	
Castiza	*Sister to Vindici*
Her Mother	
The Duchess	
Lords	
Judges	
Attendants	
Executioner &c.	

THE
REUENGERS TRAGÆDIE.

ACT I. SCÆ. I.

Enter VINDICI, *the Duke, Dutchesse,* LUSSURIOSO *her sonne,* SPURIO *the bastard, with a traine, passe ouer the Stage with Torch-light.*

Vindici.

UKE, royall letcher, goe, gray hayrde adultery,
And thou his sonne as impious steept as hee:
And thou his bastard, true-begott in euill :
And thou his Dutchesse that will doe with Diuill,
Foure ex'lent Characters.—O, that marrow-lesse age
Should stuffe the hollow Bones with dambd desires,
And 'stead of heate kindle infernall fires

Within the spend-thrift veynes of a drye Duke,
A parcht and juicelesse luxur. O God! One
That has scarce bloud inough to liue upon,—
And hee to ryot it like a sonne and heyre?
O the thought of that
Turnes my abused heart-strings into fret.
Thou sallow picture of my poysoned loue,
My studies ornament, thou shell of Death,
Once the bright face of my betrothed Lady,
When life and beauty naturally fild out
These ragged imperfections;
When two heauen-pointed Diamonds were set
In those unsightly rings; then 'twas a face
So farre beyond the artificiall shine
Of any woman's bought complexion,
That the uprightest man (if such there be,
That sinne but seauen times a day) broke custom
And made up eight with looking after her.
Oh, she was able to ha' made a Usurer's sonne
Melt all his patrimony in a kisse,
And what his father fiftie yeares told
To haue consumde, and yet his sute beene cold.
But oh accursed Pallace!

Thee, when thou wert appareld in thy flesh,
The old Duke poyson'd,
Because thy purer part would not consent
Unto his palsey-lust; for old men lust-full
Do show like young men angry, eager, violent,
Outbidden, like their limited performances.
O ware an old man hot, and vicious!
Age as in gold in lust is couetous.
Vengence, thou murder's Quit-rent, and whereby
Thou show'st thy selfe Tennant to Tragedy,
Oh keepe thy day, houre, minute, I beseech,
For those thou hast determind. Hum! who ere knew
Murder unpayd? Faith, giue Reuenge her due;
Sha's kept touch hetherto;—be merry, merry;—
Aduance thee, O thou terror to fat folkes
To haue their costly three-pilde flesh worne off
As bare as this;—for banquets, ease, and laughter
Can make great men, as greatnesse goes by clay;
But wise men little are more great then they.

Enter his brother HIPPOLITO.

Hip. Still sighing o're deaths vizard?

Vind. Brother, welcome.

    What comfort bringst thou? how go things a Court?

Hip. In silke and siluer, brother: neuer brauer.

Vind. Puh,

    Thou playst upon my meaning; pree-thee say
    Has that bald Madam, Opportunity,
    Yet thought upon 's? Speake, are we happy yet
    Thy wrongs and mine are for one scabberd fit.

Hip. It may proue happinesse.

Vind. What is't may proue?
    Giue me to taste.

Hip. Giue me your hearing, then.
    You know my place at Court?

Vind. Aye; the Dukes Chamber.
    But 'tis a maruaile thou'rt not turnd out yet!

Hip. Faith, I have beene shoou'd at, but 'twas still my hap
    To hold by 'th Duchesse' skirt; you gesse at that,—
    Whome such a Coate keepes up can nere fall flat.
    But to the purpose.
    Last euening, predecessor unto this,

The Duke's sonne warily enquir'd for me,
Whose pleasure I attended: he began,
By policy to open and unhuske me
About the time and common rumour:
But I had so much wit to keepe my thoughts
Up in their built houses, yet afforded him
An idle satisfaction without danger.
But the whole ayme, and scope of his intent
Ended in this, conjuring me in priuate
To seeke some strange-digested fellow forth:
Of ill-contented nature, either disgracst
In former times, or by new groomes displacst
Since his Step-mother's nuptialls; such a bloud,
A man that were for euill onely good;
To giue you the true word,—some base coyned
   Pander!

Vind. I reach you, for I know his heate is such,
Were there as many Concubines as Ladies
He would not be contaynd, he must flie out:
I wonder how ill-featur'd, vile-proportion'd
That one should be, if she were made for woman,
Whom at the Insurrection of his lust
He would refuse for once? Heart, I thinke none

    Next to a skull, tho' more unsound than one.
    Each face he meetes he strongly doates upon.

Hip. Brother, y'aue truly spoke him.
    He knowes not you, but I'le sweare you know him

Vind. And therefore I'le put on that knaue for once,
    And be a right man then, a man a'th Time;
    For to be honest is not to be i'th' world.
    Brother, I'le be that strange-composed fellow.

Hip. And I'le prefer you, brother.

Vind. Go to then,—
    The small'st aduantage fattens wronged men
    It may point out occasion; if I meete her,
    I'll hold her by the fore-top fast ynough;
    Or like the *French Moale* heaue up haire and all
    I haue a habit that wil fit it quaintly.
    Here comes our Mother. *Hip.* And sister.

Vind. We must quoyne.
    Women are apt, you know, to take false money,
    But I dare stake my soule for these two creatures
    Onely excuse excepted, that they'le swallow,
    Because their sexe is easie in beleefe.

[*Enter the* MOTHER *and* CASTIZA.]

Moth. What newes from Court, sonne Carlo?

Hip. Faith, Mother,
  'Tis whispered there the Duchesse' yongest sonne
  Has playd a Rape on Lord Antonio's wife.

Moth. On that relligious Lady!

Cast. Royal-blood monster!
  He deserues to die,
  If Italy had no more hopes but he.

Vind. Sister, y'aue sentenc'd most direct and true;
  The Lawe's a woman, and would she were you.
  Mother, I must take leaue of you.

Moth. Leaue for what?

Vin. I intend speedy trauaile.

Hip. That he does, Madam. *Mo.* Speedy indeed!

Vind. For since my worthy father's funerall,
  My life's unnaturally to me, e'en compeld
  As if I liu'd now when I should be dead.

Moth. Indeed, he was a worthy Gentleman,
  Had his estate beene fellow to his mind.

Vind. The Duke did much deject him.

Moth. Much?

Vind. Too much!
And though disgrace oft smotherd in his spirit,
When it would mount, surely I think hee dyed
Of discontent,—the nobleman's consumption.

Moth. Most sure he did!

Vind. Did he, 'lack?——you know all,
You were his mid-night secretary.

Moth. No.
He was too wise to trust me with his thoughts.

Vind. Y' faith then, father, thou wast wise indeed,—
"Wiues are but made to go to bed and feede."
Come, mother, sister: you'll bring me onward,
brother?

Hip. I will.

Vind. I'll quickly turne into another. *Exeunt.*

[SCENE II.]

Enter the old Duke, LUSSURIOSO *his sonne, the Duchesse: the Bastard, the Duchesse two sonnes* AMBITIOSO *and* SUPERUACUO; *the third her youngest brought out with Officers for the Rape: Two Judges.*

Duke. Duchesse, it is your youngest sonne; we're sory

His violent Act has e'en drawne bloud of honor,
And stain'd our honors;
Throwne inck upon the for-head of our state,
Which enuious spirits will dip their pens into
After our death,—and blot us in our Toombes.
For that which would seeme treason in our liues
Is laughter when we're dead. Who dares now whisper
That dares not then speake out, and e'en proclaime,
With lowd words and broad pens our closest shame?

Jud. Your grace hath spoke like to your siluer yeares
Full of confirmed grauity;—for what is it to haue
A flattering false insculption on a Toombe,
And in men's hearts reproch? The bowel'd Corps,
May be seard in; but, (with free tongue I speake)
The faults of great men through their searde clothes breake.

Duk. They do, we're sory for 't. It is our fate
To liue in feare, and die to liue in hate:
I leaue him to your sentance. Doome him, Lords:
The fact is great, whilst I sit by and sigh.

Duch. My gratious Lord, I pray, be mercifull.

       Although his trespasse far exceed his yeares,
       Thinke him to be your owne as I am yours,
       Call him not sonne in law: the law I feare
       Will fall too soone upon his name and him:
       Temper his fault with pitty.

Luss. Good my Lord—
       Then twill not taste so bitter and unpleasant
       Upon the Judge's pallat; for offences
       Gilt ore with mercy, show like fayrest women,
       Good onely for their beauties, which washt off
       No sin is uglier.

Amb. I beseech your grace,
       Be soft and mild, let not Relentesse Law
       Looke with an iron for-head on our brother.

Spu. He yeelds small comfort yet; 'hope he shall di
       And if a bastard's wish might stand in force,
       Would all the court were turn'd into a corse.

Duc. No pitty yet? must I rise fruitlesse then?
       A wonder in a woman; are my knees,
       Of such lowe mettall that without Respect——

1. *Judg.* Let the offender stand forth,
       Tis the Duke's pleasure that Impartiall Doome
       Shall take fast hold of his uncleane attempt.

A Rape! why tis the very core of lust,
Double Adultery.

Juni. So Sir.

2. *Jud.* And which was worse,
Committed on the Lord Antonio's wife,
That generall-honest Lady. Confesse my Lord,
What mou'd you to 't?

Juni. Why flesh and blood my Lord.
What should moue men unto a woman else?

Luss. O do not jest thy doome; trust not an axe
Or sword too far; the Law is a wise serpent
And quickly can beguile thee of thy life.
Tho' marriage onely has made thee my brother,
I loue thee so far, play not with thy Death.

Juni. I thanke you, 'troth; good admonitions, 'faith,
If I'd the grace now to make use of them.

1. *Jud.* That Ladye's name has spread such a faire wing
Ouer all Italy; that if our Tongs
Were sparing toward the Fact, Judgment it selfe
Would be condemned, and suffer in mens' thoughts.

Juni. Well then, 'tis done, and it would please me well
Were it to doe agen. Sure she's a Goddesse,

For I'd no power to see her, and to liue;
It falls out true in this, for I must die.
Her beauty was ordaynd to be my scaffold,
And yet me thinks I might be easier 'sess'd,
My fault being sport, let me but die in jest.

1. *Jud.* This be the sentence ;—

Dut. O keep't upon your Tongue, let it not slip;
Death too soone steales out of a Lawyer's lip.
Be not so cruell-wise.

1. *Judg.* Your Grace must pardon us,
'Tis but the Justice of the Lawe.

Dut. The Lawe
Is growne more subtill than a woman should be

Spu. Now, now he dies; rid 'em away.

Dut. O what it is to haue a old-coole Duke,
To bee as slack in tongue, as in performance.

1. *Judg.* Confirm'd, this be the doome irreuocable.

Dut. Oh!

1. *Judg.* To-morrow early——

Dut. Pray be a bed, my Lord.

1. *Judg.* Your Grace much wrongs your selfe.

Ambi. No, 'tis that tongue;
    Your too much right does do us too much wrong.

1. *Judg.* Let that offender——

Dut. Liue, and be in health.

1. *Jud.* Be on a Scaffold—

Duke. Hold, hold, my Lord.

Spu. Pox on't,
    What makes my Dad speake now?

Duke. We will defer the judgement till next sitting.
    In the meane time let him be kept close prisoner:
    Guard, beare him hence.

Ambi. Brother, this makes for thee;
    Feare not, wee'll haue a trick to set thee free.

Juni. Brother, I will expect it from you both;
    And in that hope I rest.

Super. Farewell, be merry.   *Exit with a garde.*

Spu. Delay'd, defer'd; nay, then, if judgement haue cold bloud,
    Flattery and bribes will kill it.

Duke. About it then, my Lords, with your best powers;—
    More serious businesse calls upon our houres.

    Manent Executioner and Duchess.

Dut. Was't euer knowne step-Dutchesse was so milde,
    And calme as I? Some now would plot his death,
    With easie Doctors, those loose-liuing men,
    And make his witherd Grace fall to his Graue,
    And keepe Church better.
    Some second wife would doe this, and dispatch
    Her double-loathed Lord at meate or sleepe.
    Indeed 'tis true an old man's twice a childe,—
    Mine cannot speake; one of his single words
    Would quite haue freed my yongest, deerest, sonne
    From death or durance, and haue made him walke
    With a bold foote upon the thornie law,
    Whose Prickles should bow under him; but 'tis
      not,
    And therefore wedlock-faith shall be forgot.
    I'll kill him in his fore-head; hate there feede;
    That wound is deepest tho' it neuer bleed.
    And here comes hee whom my heart points unto,
    His bastard sonne, but my loue's true-begot.
    Many a wealthy letter haue I sent him,
    Sweld up with Jewels; and the timorous man
    Is yet but coldly kinde.
    That Jewel's mine that quiuers in his eare,

Mocking his Maister's chilnesse and vaine feare.
Ha's spide me now.   *Enter* SPURIO.

Spu. Madame, your Grace so priuate?
My duety on your hand.

Dut. Upon my hand, sir? troth, I thinke you'd feare
To kisse my hand too, if my lip stood there.

Spi. Witnesse I would not, Madam.

Dut. Tis a wonder;
For ceremonie has made many fooles.
It is as easie way unto a Dutchesse,
As to a Hatted-dame, (if her loue answer)—
But that by timorous honors, pale respects,
Idle degrees of feare, men make their wayes
Hard of themselues.——What haue you thought
of me?

Spu. Madam, I euer thinke of you in duty—
Regard and ——

Dut. Puh! upon my loue, I meane.

Spu. I would 'twere loue, but 'tis a fowler name
Than lust. You are my father's wife; your Grace
may gesse now,
What I could call it.

Dut. Why, th'art his sonne but falsëly;
  Tis a hard question whether he begot thee.

Spu. 'I faith, 'tis true too; I'm an uncertaine man,
  Of more uncertaine woman. May be his groome
    'ath' stable begot me; you know I know not.
    Hee could ride a horse well, (a shrowd suspi-
    tion, marry)——hee was wondrous tall, hee had
    his length, i'faith, for peeping ouer halfe-shut
    holy-day windowes.
  Men would desire him light; when he was a foote,
  He made a goodly show under a Pent-house,—
  And when he rid, his Hatt would check the signes,
  And clatter Barbers' Basons.

Dut. Nay, set you a horse back once,
  You'll nere light off.

Spu. Indeed I am a beggar.

Dut. That's more the signe thou'rt Great.—But to our
    loue.
  Let it stand firme both in thy thought and minde.
  That the Duke was thy Father,—as no doubt then
  Hee bid faire for't,—thy injurie is the more.
  For had hee cut thee a right Diamond,

      Thou had'st beene next set in the Duke-dome's
          Ring,
      When his worne selfe, like Age's easie slaue,
      Had dropt out of the Collet into th' Graue.
      What wrong can equall this? canst thou be tame
      And thinke uppon't?

Spu. No, mad and thinke upon't.

Dut. Who would not be reueng'd of such a father,
      E'en in the worst way? I would thanke that sinne,
      That could most injure him, and bee in league
          with it.
      O what a griefe 'tis, that a man should liue
      But once 'ith' world, and then to liue a Bastard,
      The curse a' the wombe, the theefe of Nature,
      Begot against the seauenth commandement,
      Halfe damn'd in the conception, by the justice
      Of that unbribed euerlasting law.

Spu. O, I'd a hot-back'd Diuill to my father.

Dut. Would not this mad e'en patience, make bloud
          rough?
      Who but an Eunuch would not sinne? his bed
      By one false minute disinherited.

Spu. Aye, there's the vengeance that my birth was wrapt
in.
I'll be reuenged for all. Now, hate, begin:
I'll call foule Incest but a Veniall sinne.

Dut. Cold still! in vaine then must a Dutchesse woo i

Spu. Madam, I blush to say what I will doo.

Dut. Thence flew sweet comfort. Earnest, and farewel

Spu. Oh one incestuous kiss picks open hell.

Dut. 'Faith now, old Duke, my vengeance shall reach
high:
I'll arme thy brow with woman's Herauldie. *Exit*

Spu. Duke, thou didst do me wrong, and by thy Act
Adultery is my nature.
'Faith if the truth were knowne I was begot
After some gluttonous dinner; some stirring dish
Was my first father; when deepe healths wen
round,
And Ladies' cheeks were painted red with Wine,
Their tongues as short and nimble as their heeles
Uttering words sweet and thick, and when they
rose
Were merrily dispos'd to fall agen.

In such a whisp'ring and with-drawing houre,
When base male-Bawdes kept Centinell at stairehead,
Was I stol'n softly.   Oh! damnation met
The sinne of feasts, drunken adultery.
I feele it swell me; my reuenge is just,
I was begot in impudent Wine and Lust.
Step mother, I consent to thy desires;
I loue thy mischiefe well, but I hate thee,
And those three Cubs thy sonnes, wishing confusion
Death and disgrace may be their Epitaphs.
As for my brother, the Dukes onely sonne,
Whose birth is more beholding to report
Than mine, and yet perhaps as falsely sowne,
(Women must not be trusted with their owne)
I'll loose my dayes upon him, hate-all I.
Duke, on thy browe I'll drawe my Bastardie;
For indeed a bastard by nature should make cuckolds,
Because he is the sonne of a Cuckold-maker.

Exit.

[SCENE III.]

Enter VINDICI *and* HIPPOLITO. VINDICI *in disguise to attend* LUSSURIOSO *the Duke's sonne.*

Vind. What, brother? am I farre inough from myselfe?

Hip. As if another man had beene sent whole
Into the world, and none wist how he came.

Vind. It will confirme me bould, the child a' th' Court—
Let blushes dwell i' th' Country.   Impudence;
Thou Goddesse of the pallace, Mistris of Mistresses,
To whom the costly-perfum'd people pray,
Strike thou my fore-head into dauntlesse Marble;
Mine eyes to steady Saphires.   Turne my visage,
And if I must needes glow, let me blush inward,
That this immodest season may not spy
That scholler in my cheekes, foole bashfullnes—
That Maide in the old time, whose flush of Grace
Would neuer suffer her to get good cloaths.
Our Maides are wiser; and are lesse asham'd,
Saue *Grace* the bawde I seldome heare Grace nam'd.

Hip. Nay, brother, you reach out a'th' Verge now. 'Sfoote,
    The Dukes sonne! settle your lookes.

Vind. Pray let me not be doubted

Hip. My Lord.

Luss. Hipolito—be absent—leaue us.

Hip. My Lord after long search, wary inquiries,
    And politick siftings I made choice of yon fellow,
    Whom I gesse rare for many deepe employments.
    This our age swims within him, and if Time
    Had so much hayre, I should take him for Time.
    He is so neere kinne to this present minute.

Luss. 'Tis inough.
    We thanke thee; yet words are but great men's blanckes;
    Gold, tho' it be dumb, does utter the best thankes.

Hip. Your plenteous honor! An ex'lent fellow, my Lord.   *Exit* HIPPOLITO.

Luss. So, giue us leaue; Welcome, bee not far off, we must bee better acquainted. Tush; be bould with us,—thy hand.

Vind. With all my heart i'faith ! How dost, sweete
    Muskcat,
    When shall we lie togither ?

Luss. Wondrous Knaue !
    Gather him into bouldnesse ; 'Sfoote, the slaue's
    Already as familiar as an Ague
    And shakes me at his pleasure. Friend, I can
    Forget my selfe in priuate, but else where
    I pray, do you remember me.

Vind. Oh, very well, sir—; I conster my selfe sawcy.

Luss. What hast beene ?
    Of what profession ?

Vind. A bone-setter. *Luss.* A bone-setter ?

Vind. A bawde, my Lord ;
    One that setts bones togither.

Luss. Notable bluntnesse !
    Fit, fit for me, e'en traynd up to my hand !
    Thou hast beene Scriuener to much knauery then.

Vind. S'foote, to abundance, sir : I haue beene witnesse
    To the surrenders of a thousand virgins :
    And not so little ;
    I haue seene Patrimonies washt a' peices,

  Fruit-fields turnd into bastards,
  And in a world of Acres
  Not so much dust due to the heire t'was left to,
  As would well grauell a petition.

Luss. Fine villaine! troth, I like him wondrously
  Hee's e'en shapt for my purpose. Then thou knowst
  I'th' world strange lust.

Vind. O Dutch lust! fulsome lust!
  Druncken procreation which begets so many drunckards,
  Some father dreads not (gonne to bedde in wine)
   To slide from the mother
  And cling the daughter in law;
  Some Uncles are adulterous with their Neeces,
  Brothers with brothers' wiues; O howre of Incest!
  Any kin now, next to the Rim' a'th' sister
  Is man's meate in these dayes; and in the morning
  When they are up and drest, and their maske on
  Who can perceiue this, saue that eternal eye
  That sees through flesh and all? Well,—if any thing be damn'd
  It will be twelue a'clock at night,—that twelue

          Will never 'scape :
          It is the *Judas* of the howers, wherein
          Honest saluation is betray'd to sin.

Luss. Introth, it is too—but let this talke glide—
          It is our bloud to erre, tho' hell gap't wide ;
          Ladies know Lucifer fell, yet still are proude,
          Now, sir, wert thou as secret as thou'rt subtil
          And deepely fadom'd into all estates,
          I would embrace thee for a neere employment,
          And thou shoul'dst swell in money, and be able
          To make lame beggars crouch to thee.

Vind. My Lord,
          Secret ! I nere had that disease a'th' mother,
          I praise my father. Why are men made close
          But to keepe thoughts in best ? I grant you this
          Tell but some woman a secret ouer night,
          Your doctor may finde it in the vrinall i'th'
              morning.
          But, my Lord——

Luss. So, thou'rt confirmd in mee
          And thus I enter thee.   *Gives him money.*

Vind. This Indian Diuill

Will quickly enter any man but a Usurer;
He preuents that by entering the diuill first.

Luss. Attend me. I am past my depth in lust,
And I must swim or drowne. All my desires
Are leueld at a Virgin not far from court,
To whom I haue conuey'd by Messenger
Many waxt Lines full of my neatest spirit,
And jewells that were able to rauish her
Without the helpe of man; all which and more
Shee, foolish chast, sent back the messengers
Receiuing frownes for answeres.

Vind. Possible!
Tis a rare Phœnix, whosoere she bee,
If your desires be such, she so repugnant,
In troth my Lord I'd be reueng'd and marry her.

Luss. Tush! the doury of her bloud and of her fortunes
Are both too meane,—good inough to be bad with.
I'm one of that number can defend
Marriage is good; yet rather keepe a friend.
Giue me my bed by stealth—there's true delight
What breeds a loathing in't but night by night?

Vind. A very fine relligion!

Luss. Therefore thus ;
    I'll trust thee in the businesse of my heart,
    Because I see thee well experienc't
    In this Luxurious day wherein we breathe.
    Go thou, and with a smooth enchaunting tongue
    Bewitch her eares, and Couzen her of all Grace ;
    Enter upon the portion of her soule
    Her honour, which she calls her chastity,
    And bring it into expence ; for honesty
    Is like a stock of money lay'd to sleepe
    Which, nere so little broke, doe's neuer keep. .

Vind. You haue giu't the Tang i'faith my Lord,
    Make knowne the Lady to me, and my braine
    Shall swell with strange Inuention. I will moue it
    Till I expire with speaking and drop downe,
    Without a word to saue me,—but I'll worke——

Luss. We thanke thee, and will raise thee. Receiue her name, it is the only daughter to Madame Gratiana, the late widdow.

Vind. Oh my sister! my sister! [Aside] *Luss.* Why dost walke aside ?

Vind. My Lord, I was thinking how I might begin ;

As thus, "oh Ladie"—or twenty hundred deuices;
Her very bodkin will put a man in.

Luss. Aye, or the wagging of her haire.

Vind. No, that shall put you in, my Lord.

Luss. Shal't? Why, content. Dost know the daughter then?

Vind. O, ex'lent well by sight.

Luss. That was her brother
That did prefer thee to us.

Vind. My Lord, I think so:
I knew I had seene him some where.

Luss. And therefore, prythee, let thy heart to him
Be as a Virgin, close. *Vind.* Oh, my good Lord.

Luss. We may laugh at that simple age within him.

Vind. Ha! ha! ha!

Luss. Himselfe being made the subtill instrument
To winde up a good fellow.

Vind. That's I, my Lord.

Luss. That's thou.
To entice and worke his sister.

Vind. A pure nouice! *Luss.* 'Twas finely manag'd.

Vind. Gallantly carried.

A pretty perfum'd villaine.

Luss. I'ue bethought me.

If she prooue chast still, and immoueable,

Venture upon the Mother, and with giftes

As I will furnish thee, begin with her.

Vind. O fie, fie, that's the wrong end, my Lord. Tis meere impossible that a mother by any gifts should become a bawde to her owne Daughter!

Luss. Nay, then, I see thou'rt but a puny in the subtill Mistery of a woman :—why, 'tis held now no dainty dish : The name

Is so in league with age, that now adaies

It does Eclipse three quarters of a Mother.

Vind. Does't so, my Lord?

Let me alone, then, to Eclipse the fourth.

Luss. Why, well sayd. Come, I'll furnish thee; but first

Sweare to be true in all.

Vind. True.   *Luss,* Nay, but sweare.

Vind. Sweare? . . . I hope your honor little doubts my fayth.

Luss. Yet, for my humour's sake, 'cause I loue swearing.

Vind. Cause you loue swearing? 'slud I will.

Luss. Why, inough;
Ere long looke to be of better stuff.

Vind. That will do well indeed, my Lord.

Luss. Attend me. *Exit.*

Vind. Oh!
Now let me burst. I'ue eaten noble poyson.
We are made strange fellowes, brother, innocent villaines.
Wilt not be angry when thou hear'st on't, thinkst thou?
I'faith thou shalt. Sweare me to foule my sister!
Sword, I durst make a promise of him to thee;
Thou shalt dis-heire him; it shall be thine honor.
And yet, now angry froath is downe in me,
It would not proue the meanest policy
In this disguize to try the fayth of both.
Another might haue had the selfe same office,
Some slaue that would have wrought effectually,
Aye, and perhaps ore-wrought 'em. Therefore I,
Being thought trauayl'd, will apply my selfe

Unto the selfe same forme, forget my nature
As if no part about me were kin to 'em,
So touch 'em——tho' I durst almost for good
Venture my lands in heauen upon their blood.

Exit.

[SCENE IV.]

Enter the discontented Lord ANTONIO, *whose wife the Duchesses yongest Sonne rauisht—he Discouering the body of her dead to certaine Lords; and* HIPPOLITO.

L. Ant. Draw neerer, Lords, and be sad witnesses
Of a fayre comely building newly fall'n,
Being falsely undermined: violent rape
Has play'd a glorious act.   Behold, my Lords,
A sight that strikes man out of me.

Piero. That vertuous Lady!

L. Ant. Precedent for wives!

Hip. The blush of many weomen; whose chast presence
Would e'n call shame up to their cheekes
And make pale wanton sinners haue good colours.

L. Ant. Dead!

Her honor first drunke poyson, and her life,
Being fellowes in one house, did pledge her honour.

Piero. O greefe of many!

L. Ant. I mark'd not this before,
A prayer Booke the pillow to her cheeke;
This was her rich confection, and another
Plac'd in her right hand with a leafe tuckt up
Poynting to these words

Melius virtute mori, Quam per Dedecus viuere.

True and effectuall it is indeed.

Hip. My Lord, since you invite us to your sorrowes
Let's truely taste 'em, that with equall comfort
As to our selues, we may relieue your wrongs.
We have greefe too, that yet walkes without tongue

Curæ leues loquuntur, Maiores stupent.

L. Ant. You deale with truth, my Lord.
Lend me but your Attentions, and I'll cut
Long greefe into short words. Last reuelling night,
When Torch-light made an artificiall noone
About the Court, some Courtiers in the maske

Putting on better faces than their owne,
Being full of frawde and flattery—amongst whome
The Duchesse's yongest sonne (that moth to honor)
Fill'd up a Roome; and, with long lust to eat
Into my wearing, amongst all the Ladyes,
Singled out that deare forme, who euer liu'd
As cold in Lust as shee is now in death,
(Which that step-Duches' Monster knew too well.)
And therefore in the height of all the reuells,
When Musick was heard lowdest, Courtiers busiest,
And Ladies great with laughter;—O Vitious minute!
Unfit, but for relation, to be spoke of,—
Then, with a face more impudent then his vizard,
He harried her amidst a throng of Panders,
That liue uppon damnation of both kindes,
And fed the rauenous vulture of his lust.—
O death to thinke on't! She, her honor forc'd
Deem'd it a nobler dowry for her name
To die with poyson, then to liue with shame.

Hip. A wondrous Lady, of rare fire compact.
Sha's made her name an Empresse by that act.

Piero. My Lord, what iudgement followes the offender?

L. Ant. 'Faith, none my Lord : it cooles and is defer'd.

Piero. Delay the doome for rape?

L. Ant. O, you must note who 'tis should die ;
    The Duchesse' sonne : shee'll looke to be a sauer,
    Judgment in this age is near kin to fauour.

Hip. Nay, then, step forth thou Bribelesse officer!
    I bind you all in steele to bind you surely.
    Here let your oaths meet to be kept and payd,
    Which else will sticke like rust and shame the
        blade.
    Strengthen my vow, that if, at the next sitting,
    Jndgment speake all in gold, and spare the bloud
    Of such a serpent,—e'en before their seats—
    To let his soule out, which long time was found
    Guilty in heauen.

All. We sweare it, and will act it.

L. Ant. Kind Gentlemen, I thanke you in mine Ire.

Hip. 'Twere pitty
    The ruins of so faire a Monument
    Should not be dipt in the defacer's bloud.

Piero. Her funerall shall be wealthy, for her name

Merits a toombe of pearle.   My Lord Antonio,
For this time wipe your Lady from your eyes;
No doubt our greefe and youres may one day
    court it,
When we are more familiar with Reuenge.

L. Ant. That is my comfort, Gentlemen, and I joy
In this one happines aboue the rest,
Which will be call'd a miracle at last;
That being an old man, I'd a wife so chaste.

Exeunt.

ACTUS. 2. SCÆ. I.

Enter CASTIZA *the sister*.

Cast. How hardly shall that mayden be beset
   Whose onely fortunes are her constant thoughts!
   That has no other childe's-part but her honor,
   That keepes her lowe and empty in estate.
   Maydes and their honors are like poore beginners—
   Were not sinne rich there would be fewer sinners.
   Why had not vertue a revennue? well,
   I know the cause,—'twou'd haue impouerish'd hell.
   How now Dondolo? *Enter* DONDOLO.

Don. Madonna there is one as they say a thing of flesh and blood,—a man I take him by his beard—that would very desireously mouth to mouth with you.

Cast. What's that?

Don. Show his teeth in your company.

Cast. I understand thee not.

Don. Why, speake with you, Madonna.

Cast. Why say so, mad-man, and cut off a great deale of
dirty way. Had it not beene better spoke in
ordinary words, that one would speake with me?

Don. Ha! ha! that's as ordinary as two shillings. I
would striue a litle to show my selfe in my
place; a Gentleman-usher scornes to use the
Phrase and fancie of a seruingman.

Cast. Yours be your own sir; go, direct him hither,
I hope some happy tidings from my brother
That lately trauayl'd, whome my soule affects.
Here he comes.

Enter VINDICI *her brother disguised.*

Vind. Lady, the best of wishes to your sexe
Faire skins and new gownes.

Cast. Oh they shall thanke you sir.
Whence this?

Vind. Oh from a deere and worthy friend
Mighty——   *Cast.* From whome?

Vind. The Duke's sonne.

Cast. Receiue that.   *A boxe 'ath' eare to her brother.*
I swore I would put anger in my hand

And passe the Virgin limits of my selfe
To him that next appear'd in that base office
To be his sinnes' Attorney. Beare to him
That figure of my hate upon thy cheeke
Whilst 'tis yet hot, and I'll reward thee for't.
Tell him my honor shall haue a rich name
When seuerall harlots shall share his with shame.
Farewell——commend me to him in my hate.

Exit.

Vind. It is the sweetest Boxe that ere my nose came nye,
The finest drawne-worke cuffe that ere was worne;
I'll loue this blowe for euer, and this cheeke
Shall still hence forward take the wall of this.
O I'm aboue my tong: most constant sister
In this, thou hast right honorable showne
Many are call'd by their honour that haue none.
Thou art approu'd for euer in my thoughts.
It is not in the power of words to taynt thee.
And yet for the saluation of my oath,
As my resolue in that poynt, I will lay
Hard siege unto my Mother, tho' I know
A Syren's tongue could not bewitch her so.

Masse! fitly here she comes! thankes my disguize.

Madame, good afternoone.

Enter GRATIANA.

Moth. Y'are welcome sir.

Vind. The Next of Italy commends him to you,
Our mighty expectation, the Dukes sonne.

Moth. I thinke my selfe much honor'd, that he pleases
To ranck me in his thoughts.

Vind. So may you, Lady,
One that is like to be our suddaine Duke,—
The Crowne gapes for him euery tide and then—
Commander o're us all.—Do but thinke on him
How blest were they now that could pleasure him
E'en with any thing almost!

Moth. Aye, saue their honor.

Vind. Tut, one would let a little of that go too
And nere be seene in't; nere be seene in't, marke
you.
I'd winck, and let it go.

Moth. Marry, but I would not.

Vind. Marry, but I would I hope. I know you would too,
    If you'd that bloud now which you gaue your daughter,
    To her indeed 'tis, this wheele comes about.
    That man that must be all this, perhaps ere morning
    (For his white father does but moulde away)
    Has long desir'd your daughter.

Moth. Desir'd?

Vind. Nay, but heare me.
    He desires now, that will command hereafter.
    Therefore be wise, I speake as more a friend
    To you, than him. Madame I know y'are poore
    And 'lack the day! there are too many poore Ladies already.
    Why should you vex the number? 'tis despis'd,
    Liue wealthy, rightly understand the world,
    And chide away that foolish Country-girle
    Keepes company with your daughter, chastity.

Moth. Oh fie, fie! the riches of the world cannot hire a mother to such a most unnaturall taske.

Vind. No, but a thousand Angells can

Men haue no power, Angells must worke you to't.
The world descends into such base-borne euills
That forty Angells can make fourscore diuills.
There will be fooles still I perceiue,—still fooles
Would I be poore, dejected, scorn'd of greatnesse,
Swept from the Pallace, and see other daughters
Spring with the dewe a'th' Court, hauing mine owne
So much desir'd and lou'd—by the Dukes sonne?
No, I would raise my state upon her brest
And call her eyes my Tennants; I would count
My yearely maintenance upon her cheekes,
Take Coach upon her lip, and all her partes
Should keepe men after men, and I would ride
In pleasure upon pleasure.
You tooke great paines for her, once when it was,
Let her requite it now tho' it be but some,
You brought her forth, she may well bring you home.

Moth. O heauens! this ouer-comes me!

Vind. Not I hope already. [Aside.]

Moth. It is too strong for me; men know that know us,

We are so weake their words can ouerthrow us
[Aside.]
He toucht me neerely, made my vertues bate,
When his tongue struck vpon my poore estate.

Vind. I e'en quake to proceede. My spirit turnes edge
I feare me she's vnmotherd, yet I'll venture.
[Aside.]
That woman is all male whome none can Enter.
What thinke you now Lady—speake, are you wiser
What sayd aduancement to you? thus it sayd—
The daughters fall lifts up the mother's head,
Did it not Madame? but I'll sweare it does
In many places: tut, this age feares no man
'Tis no shame to be bad, because 'tis so common.

Moth. Aye, that's the comfort on't.

Vind. The comfort on't!
I keepe these best for last. Can these perswade you
To forget heauen—and——

Moth. Aye, these are they——

Vind. Oh!

Moth. That enchant our sexe
These are the means that gouerne our affections—
that woman

Will not be troubled with the mother long,
That see the comfortable shine of you.
I blush to thinke what for your sakes I'll do!

Vind. O suffring heauen! with thy inuisible finger [Aside.]
E'en at this instant turne the pretious side
Of both mine eye-balls inward, not to see my selfe.

Moth. Looke you sir.   *Vind.* Holla!

Moth. Let this thanke your paines.

Vind. O y'are kind, Madame.

Moth. I'll see how I can moue.

Vind. Yours words will sting.

Moth. If she be still chast, I'll nere call her mine.

Vind. Spoke truer then you meant it.

Moth. Daughter Castiza.

Cast. Madam.

Vind. O shee's yonder—— Meete her [Aside.]
Troupes of celestiall Soldiers, gard her heart.
Yon dam has deuills enough to take her part.

Cast. Madam, what makes yon euill-offic'd man
In presence of you?

Moth. Why?

Cast. He lately brought
    Immodest writing sent from the Dukes sonne,
    To tempt me to dishonorable Act.

Moth. Dishonorable Act!——good honorable foole
    That wouldst be honest 'cause thou wouldst be so,
    Producing no one reason but thy will
    And t'has a good report, prettely commended
    But pray by whome? meane people, ignorant
        people;
    The better sort I'm sure cannot abide it.
    And by what rule shouldst we square out our liues
    But by our better actions? Oh, if thou knew'st
    What 'twere to lose it, thou would neuer keepe it
    But there's a cold curse laid upon all Maydes,
    Whilst others clip the Sunne, they clasp the shades
    Virginity is paradise lockt up
    You cannot come by your selues without fee
    And 'twas decreed that man should keepe the key
    Deny aduancement! Treasure! the Dukes sonne!

Cast. I cry your mercy, Lady, I mistooke you,—
    Pray did you see my Mother? Which way went you?
    Pray God I haue not lost her.

Vind. Prittily put by.

Moth. Are you as proud to me as coye to him?
Doe you not know me now?

Cast. Why are you shee?
The world's so changed one shape into another,
It is a wise childe now that knowes her mother.

Vind. Most right i'faith.

Moth. I owe your cheeke my hand
For that presumption now, but I'll forget it.
Come, you shall leaue those childish 'hauiours
And understand your Time, Fortunes flow to you
What will you be a Girle?
If all fear'd drowning that spye waues a shoare,
Gold would grow rich and all the Marchants poore.

Cast. It is a pritty saying of a wicked one; but me thinkes now
It does not show so well out of your mouth,
Better in his.

Vind. 'Faith, bad inough in both
Were I in earnest, as Ile seeme no lesse.
                              [Aside.]
I wonder Lady your owne mother's words

Cannot be taken, nor stand in full force.
'Tis honestie you urge,—what's honestie?
'Tis but heauen's beggar. And what woman is so
   foolish to keepe honesty
And be not able to keepe her-selfe? No,
Times are growne wiser, and will keep lesse charge.
A Maide that has small portion now intends
To breake up house, and liue upon her friends.
How blest are you, you haue happinesse alone,
Others must fall to thousands, you to one
Sufficient in him-selfe to make your fore-head
Dazle the world with Jewels, and petitionary people
Start at your presence.

Moth. Oh, if I were yong, I should be rauisht.

Cast. Aye, to lose your honor.

Vind. 'Slid how can you lose your honor
   To deale with my Lords Grace?
   Hee'll adde more honour to it by his Title,—
   Your mother will tell you how.

Moth. That I will.

Vind. O thinke upon the pleasure of the Pallace
   Secured ease and state; the stirring meates

    Ready to moue out of the dishes, that e'en now
     quicken when they're eaten
    Banquets abroad by Torch-light, musicks, sports
    Bare-headed vassailes that had nere the fortune
    To keepe on their owne Hats, but let hornes
     weare 'em.
    Nine Coaches waiting——hurry, hurry, hurry.—

Cast. Aye, to the Diuill.

Vind. Aye, to the Diuill—to the Duke, by my faith.

Moth. Aye, to the Duke, daughter you'd scorne to thinke
    a'th'
    Diuill, an you were there once.

Vind. True, for most there are as proud as he, for his
    heart i'faith.
    Who'd sit at home in a neglected roome,
    Dealing her short-liu'd beauty to the pictures
    That are as uselesse as old men? When those,
    Poorer in face and fortunes than herselfe,
    Walke with a hundred Acres on their backs,
    Faire Meadowes cut into Greene fore parts—oh
    It was the greatest blessing euer happened to
     woman

When Farmers' sonnes agreed, and met agen
To wash their hands, and come up Gentlemen.
The common wealth has flourisht, euer since
Lands that were mete by the Rod,—that labor's spar'd,—
Taylors ride downe and measure 'em by the yeard.
Faire trees, those comely fore-tops of the Field
Are cut to maintaine head-tires, much untold.
All thriues but chastity; she lyes a cold.
Nay shall I come neerer to you? marke but this
Why are so few honest women, but because 'tis the poorer profession. That's accounted best, that's best followed: least in trade, least in fashion and that's not honesty, beleeue it, and doe but note the loue and deiected price of it.

Lose but a pearle, we search but cannot brooke it,
But that once gone, who is so mad to looke it?

Mother. Troth, he sayes true.

Cast. False, I defie you both.
I haue endur'd you with an eare of fire,
Your Tongues haue struck hotte yrons on my face.
Mother, come from that poysonous woman there.

Mother. Where?

4—2

Cast. Do you not see her? Shee's too inward then,
  ⎰ Slaue perish in thy office, you heauvens please
  ⎱ Hence forth to make the Mother a disease
  ⎱ Which first begins with me, yet I've out-gone you.
                                                    Exit.

Vind. O Angels clap your wings upon the skyes,
  And giue this Virgin Christall plaudities

Moth. Peeuish, coy, foolish ;—but returne this answer
  My Lord shall be most welcome, when his pleasure
  Conducts him this way, I will sway my owne.
  Women with women can worke best alone *Exit.*

Vind. Indeed I'll tell him so.
  O more unciuill more unnaturall
  Then those base titled creatures that looke downe-
    ward.
  Why does not heauen turne black, or with a frowne
  Undoo the world? why does not the earth start up
  And strike the sinnes that tread uppon't—oh
  →Wert not for gold and women there would be no
    damnation
  Hell would looke like a Lord's great Kitchin
    without fire in't,
  But t'was decreed before the world began,

That they should be the hookes to catch at man
                                          . *Exit.*

[SCENE II.]

Enter Lussurioso *with* Hippolito Vindicie's *brother.*

Luss. I much applaud thy judgement, thou art well read
   in a fellow,
And t'is the deepest Arte to studie man.
I know this, which I neuer learnt in schooles,
The world's diuided into knaues and fooles.

Hip. Knaue in your face my Lord,——Behind your
   back——

Luss. And I much thanke thee that thou hast preferd
A fellow of discourse well mingled,
And whose braine Time hath season'd.

Hip. True, my Lord
We shall finde season once I hope. O villaine
To make such an unnaturall slave of me—but—
                                          [Aside.]

Luss. Masse, here he comes

Hip. And now shall I haue free leaue to depart

Luss. Your absence—leaue us.

Hip. Are not my thoughts true? [Aside]
    I must remooue, but brother you may stay
    Heart, we are both made Bawdes a new found way. *Exit.*

Luss. Now we're an euen number; a third man's dangerous
    Especially her brother, say, be free,
    Haue I a pleasure toward? *Vind.* Oh my Lord.

Luss. Rauish me in thine answer, art thou rare?
    Hast thou beguilde her of saluation
    And rubb'd hell ore with hunny? is she a woman?

Vind. In all but in desire

Luss. Then shee's in nothing, I bate in courage now

Vind. The words I brought
    Might well haue made indifferent honest naught.
    A right good woman in these days is changde
    Into white money, with lesse labour farre.
    Many a Maide has turn'd to Mahomet
    With easier working. I durst undertake
    Upon the pawne and forfeit of my life
    With halfe those words to flat a Puritane's wife

But she is closse and good, yet tis a doubt by this
  time; oh the mother the mother—

Luss. I neuer thought their sex had beene a wonder
  Untill this minute. What fruite from the mother?

Vind. How must I blister my soule, be forsworne
  Or shame the woman that receiu'd mee first?
  I will be true, thou liu'st not to proclaime;
  Spoke to a dying man shame has no shame
                                [Aside.]

  My Lord— *Luss.* Who's that?

Vind. Here's none but I, my Lord

Luss. What would thy haste utter?

Vind. Comfort *Luss.* Welcome

Vind. The Maide being dull, hauing no minde to travell
  Into unknowne lands, what did I straight
  But set spurs to the Mother? Golden spurs
  Will put her to a false gallop in a trice.

Luss. Is't possible that in this
  The mother should be dambd before the daughter?

Vind. Oh that's good manners, my Lord, the mother
  for her age must goe foremost you know

Luss. Thou'st spoke that true—but where comes in this comfort?

Vind. In a fine place my Lord. The unnaturall mother
Did with her tong so hard beset her honor,
That the poore foole was struck with silent wonder,
Yet still the maid, like an unlighted taper,
Was cold and chast, saue that her Mothers breath
Did blowe fire on her cheekes, the girle departed,
But the good antient Madam halfe mad, threwe me
These promising words which I tooke deepely note of—

"My Lord shall be most welcome—"

Luss. 'Faith, I thanke her—

Vind. "When his pleasure conducts him this way.'

Luss. That shall be soone, i' faith.

Vind. I will sway mine own.

Luss. Shee does the wiser, I commend her for't.

Vind. Women with women can worke best alone.

Luss. By this light, and so they can. Giue 'em their due, men are not comparable to 'em.

Vind. No, that's true, for you shall haue one woman knit

more in an hower than any man can Rauell agen in seauen and twenty yeare.

Luss. Now my desires are happy, I'll make 'em free-men now.

Thou art a pretious fellow, faith I loue thee
Be wise and make it thy reuennew—beg—leg
What office couldst thou be Ambitious for?

Vind. Office my Lord? Marry, if I might haue my wish I would haue one that was neuer beg'd yet.

Luss. Nay, then thou canst haue none.

Vind. Yes, my Lord, I could picke out another office yet, nay and keepe a horse and drab uppon't.

Luss. Pry'thee, good bluntness, tell me.

Vind. Why I would desire but this my Lord—to haue all the fees behind the Arras and all the farthingales that fall plumpe about twelue a clock at nigh upon the Rushes.

Luss. Thou'rt a mad apprehensiue knaue; dost thinke to make any great purchase of that?

Vind. O tis an unknowne thing, my Lord. I wonder t'as been mist so long.

Luss. Well, this night I'll visit her, and 'tis till then

A yeare in my desires—farewell, attend
Trust me with thy preferment. *Exit.*

Vind. My lou'd Lord.
Oh shall I kill him a'th' wrong-side now? No.
Sword thou wast neuer a back-biter yet.
I'll pierce him to his face, he shall die looking upon
  me.
Thy veines are sweld with lust, this shall unfill 'em.
Great men were Gods if beggers could not kil 'em.
Forgiue me heauen to call my mother wicked.
O lessen not my daies upon the earth,
I cannot honor her. By this I feare me
Her tongue has turned my sister unto use.
I was a villaine not to be forsworne
To this our lecherous hope, the Duke's sonne.
For Lawiers, Merchants, some diuines and all
Count beneficiall periury a sin small.
It shall go hard yet but I'll guard her honor
And keepe the portes sure.

Enter HIPPOL.

Hip. Brother how goes the world? I would know newes
  of you,
But I haue newes to tell you.

Vind. What in the name of knauery?

Hip. Knauery fayth.
    This vicious old Duke's worthily abus'd
    The pen of his bastard writes him cuckold!

Vind. His bastard?

Hip. Pray beleeue it, he and the Duchesse
    By night meete in their linnen, they have beene seene
    By staire-foote pandars!

Vind. Oh sin foule and deepe!
    Great faults are winckt at, when the Duke's asleepe.
    See, see, here comes the Spurio.

Hip. Monstrous Luxur!

Vind. Unbrac'd—two of his valiant bawdes with him.
    O there's a wicked whisper: hell is in his eare.
    Stay, let's obserue his passage.

Enter SPURIO *and Servants.*

Spu. Oh but are you sure on 't?

Ser. My Lord most sure on't, for 'twas spoke by one,
    That is most inward with the Duke's sonne's lust,
    That he intends within this houre to steale

Unto Hippolito's sister, whose chaste life
The mother has corrupted for his use.

Spu. Sweete word! sweete occasion! 'faith then, brother
I'll disinherit you in as short time
As I was when I was begot in haste.
I'll dam you at your pleasure pretious deede!
After your lust oh! 'twill be fine to bleede.
Come let our passing out be soft and wary.

            Excunt.

Vind. Marke there, there, that step now to the Duches.
This their second meeting writes the Duke Cuckold
With new additions, his horne's newly reviv'd.
Night! thou that lookst like funerall Heraulds fees
Torne downe betimes 'ith' morning, thou hangst fittly
To Grace those sins that haue no grace at all
Now 'tis full sea a bed ouer the world;
There's juggling of all sides, some that were Maides
E'en at Sun set, are now perhaps i'th' Toale-booke.
This woman, in immodest thin apparell,

Lets in her friend by water; here a Dame,
Cunning, nayles lether-hindges to a dore
To auoide proclamation.
Now Cuckolds are a quoyning apace, apace,
   apace, apace.
And careful sisters spinne that thread i'th' night
That does maintaine them and their bawdes ith
   daie.

Hip. You flow well brother.

Vind. Puh! I'm shallow yet
Too sparing and too modest. Shall I tell thee?
If euery trick were told that's dealt by night
That are few here that would not blush out right.

Hip. I am of that beleefe too.
Who's this comes?

Vind. The Dukes sonne up so late?—brother fall back
And you shall learne some mischeife. My good
   Lord

Luss. Piato! why the man I wisht for. Come
I do embrace this season for the fittest
To tast of that yong Lady. *Vind.* Heart and hell!

Hip. Dambd villaine!

Vind. I'ue no way now to crosse it, but to kill him.

Luss. Come only thou and I. *Vind.* My Lord, my Lord.

Luss. Why dost thou start us?

Vind. I'de almost forgot—the bastard—*Luss.* What of him?

Vind. This night—this houre—this minute—now—

Luss. What? what? *Vind.* Shadowes the Duchesse—

Luss. Horrible word!

Vind. And like strong poyson eates
Into the Duke your father's fore-head. *Luss.* Oh!

Vind. He makes home royall. *Luss.* Most ignoble slaue!

Vind. This is the fruite of two beds. *Luss.* I am mad.

Vind. That passage he trod warily. *Luss.* He did?

Vind. And husht his villaines euery step he tooke.

Luss. His villaines! Ile confound them.

Vind. Take 'em finely, finely now.

Luss. The Duchess Chamber-doore shall not controule mee. *Exeunt.*

Hip. Good, happy, swift, there's gunpowder 'ith' Court,
Wilde fire at mid-night, in this heedlesse fury

　　　　　He may show violence to crosse himselfe.
　　　　　I'll follow the Euent.　　　　　　　　　*Exit.*

Luss. Where is that villaine?　　　*Enter againe.*

Vind. Softly, my Lord, and you may take 'em twisted.

Luss. I care not how.

Vind. Oh! 'twill be glorious
　　　　To kill 'em doubled, when they're heapt. Be soft,
　　　　　my Lord.

Luss. Away. My spleene is not so lazy—thus and thus
　　　　I'll shake their eye-lids ope and with my sword
　　　　Shut 'em agen for euer. Villaine! Strumpet!

Dukc. You upper Guard defend us!　*Dut.* Treason!
　　　　treason!

Duke. O take mee not in sleepe! I haue great sins—I
　　　　must haue daies,
　　　　Nay months, deere sonne, with penitential heaues
　　　　To lift 'em out and not to die uncleere.
　　　　O thou wilt kill me both in heauen and here!

Luss. I am amazde to death.

Duke. Nay villaine traytor

Worse than the fowlest Epithite, now Ile gripe thee
Amongst the Lawyers—Guard !

Enter Nobles *and sonnes.*

1. *Noble.* How comes the quiet of your Grace disturbd ?

Duke. This boye, that should be my selfe after mee,
Would be my selfe before me, and in heate
Of that ambition bloudily rusht in,
Intending to depose me in my bed.

2. *Noble.* Duty and naturall loyalty for-fend !

Dut. He calld his Father villaine and me strumpet
A word that I abhorre to file my lips with.

Ambi. That was not so well done, Brother.

Luss. I am abus'd—I know there's no excuse can do me good.

Vind. Tis now good policie to be from sight.
His vicious purpose to our sisters honour
Is crost beyond our thought.

Hip. You little dreamt his Father slept heere.

Vind. O 'twas farre beyond me.
But since it fell so without fright-full word

Would he had kild him—'twould haue easde our swords.

Duke. Be comforted, our Duchesse : he shall dye.

Luss. Where's this slaue-pander now ? out of mine eye
Guiltie of this abuse. *Dissemble a flight.*

Enter SPURIO *with his villaines.*

Spu. Y'are villaines, Fablers,
You haue knaue's chins and harlot's tongues—you lie—
And I will dam you with one meale a day.

1. *Ser.* O good my Lord !

Spu. 'Sbloud you shall neuer sup.

2. *Ser.* O I beseech you sir——

Spu. To let my sword catch cold so long and misse him !

1. *Ser.* Troth my Lord 'twas his intent to meete there.

Spu. Heart, hee's yonder !
Ha ! what newes here ? is the day out 'ath 'socket
That it is Noone at Mid-night, the Court up ?
How comes the Guard so sawcie with his elbowes ?

Luss. The Bastard here ?

Nay then the truth of my intent shall out.
My Lord and Father heare me. *Duke.* Beare him hence.

Luss. I can with loyaltie excuse.

Duke. Excuse? to prison with the Villaine.
Death shall not long lag after him.

Spu. Good, i'faith then 'tis not much amisse.

Luss. Brothers, my best release lies on your tongues,
I pray perswade for mee.

Ambi. It is our duties: make your selfe sure of us.

Spu. We'll sweate in pleading.

Luss. And I may liue to thanke you. *Exeunt.*

Ambi. No, thy death shall thanke me better.

Spu. Hee's gone: I'll after him
And know his trespasse, seeme to beare a part
In all his ills, but with a Puritane heart. *Exit.*

Ambi. Now brother, let our hate and loue be wouen
So subtilly together, that in speaking one word for his life,
We may make three for his death.
The craftiest pleader gets most gold for breath.

Sup. Set on.   I'll not be farre behinde you brother.

Duke. Is't possible a sonne should bee disobedient as farre as the sword? it is the highest; he can goe no farther.

Ambi. My gratious Lord take pitty——   *Duke.* Pitty, boyes?

Ambi. Nay, wee'd be loth to mooue your Grace too much,
Wee know the trespasse is unpardonable,
Black, wicked, and unnaturall.

Sup. In a Sonne! oh Monstrous!

Ambi. Yet my Lord
A Duke's soft hand stroakes the rough head of law
And makes it lye smooth.   *Duke.* But my hand shall nere do't.

Ambi. That as you please, my Lord.

Sup. We must needs confesse
Some father would haue enterd into hate
So deadly pointed, that before his eyes
Hee would ha' seene the execution sound
Without corrupted fauor.

Ambi. But my Lord

> Your Grace may liue the wonder of all times
> In pardning that offence which neuer yet
> Had face to beg a pardon. *Duke.* Hunny, how's
> this?

Ambi. Forgiue him, good my Lord: hee's your owne sonne
And I must needs say 'twas the villier done.

Sup. Hee's the next heire——yet this true reason
gathers
None can possesse that dispossesse their fathers.
Be mercifull——

Duke. Here's no Step-mother's wit.
I'll trie 'em both upon their loue and hate.

Ambi. Be mercifull—altho'—— *Duke.* You haue pre-
uail'd.
Thy wrath like flaming waxe hath spent it selfe.
I know it was some peeuish Moone in him:
—Goe, let him bee releasd.

Sup. 'Sfoote how now Brother?

Ambi. Your Grace doth please to speake beside your
spleene.
I would it were so happy! *Duke.* Why goe; release him.

Sup. O my good Lord I know the fault's too weighty
    And full of generall loathing; too inhumaine,
    Rather by all mens voyces worthy death.

Duke. 'Tis true too. Here then, receiue this signet;
    doome shall passe.
    Direct it to the Judges; he shall dye
    Ere many dayes—make haste.

Ambi. All speed that may be.
    We could haue wisht his burthen not so sore.
    We knew your Grace did but delay before.
                        Exeunt.

Duke. Here's Enuie with a poore thin couer on't,
    Like Scarlet hid in lawne, easily spide through.
    This their ambition by the Mothers side
    Is dangerous and for safetie must be purg'd,
    I will preuent their enuies. Sure it was
    But some mistaken furie in our sonne
    Which these aspiring boyes would climbe upon.
    He shall bee released suddainly. *Enter Nobles.*

1. *Noble.* Good morning to your Grace.

Duke. Welcome my Lords.

2. *Noble.* Our knees shall take away the office of our feete
    for euer,

        Unlesse your Grace bestow a father's eye
        Upon the Clouded fortunes of your sonne,
        And in compassionate vertue grant him that
        Which make e'en meane men happy—liberty.

Duke. How seriously their loues and honors woo
        For that which I am about to pray them doo.
        Which, rise, my Lords, your knees signe his release,
        We freely pardon him.

1. *Noble.* We owe your Grace much thankes and he much duety.   *Exeunt.*

Duke. It well becomes that Judge to nod at crimes
        That does commit greater himselfe and liues,
        I may forgiue a disobedient error
        That expect pardon for adultery,
        And in my old daies am a youth in lust.
        Many a beauty haue I turnd to poyson
        In the deniall, couetous of all.
        Age hot is like a Monster to be seene :
        My haires are white and yet my sinnes are Greene.

ACT 3.

SCENE I.

Enter AMBITIOSO *and* SUPERUACUO.

Sup. Brother, let my opinion sway you once,
    I speake it for the best, to haue him die
    Surest and soonest; if the signet come
    Unto the judges' hands, why then his doome
    Will be defer'd till sittings and Court-daies
    Iuries and further.——Fayths are bought and sold
    Oths in these daies are but the skin of gold.

Ambi. In troth 'tis true too!

Sup. Then let's set by the Iudges
    And fall to the Officers, 'tis but mistaking
    The Duke our father's meaning, and where he nam'd
    ' Ere many daies', 'tis but forgetting that
    And haue him die i' th' morning.

Ambi. Excellent!
    Then am I heire——Duke in a minute!

Sup. Nay,

    An he were once pufft out, here is a pinne
    Should quickly prick your bladder.

Ambi. Blest occasion.
    He being packt, wee'll haue some trick and wile
    To winde our yonger brother out of prison
    That lies in for the Rape, the Ladie's dead
    And people's thoughts will soone be buried.

Sup. We may with safty do't and liue and feede,
    The Duchesse' sonnes are too proud to bleed.

Ambi. We are, yfaith, to say true.—Come let's not linger.
    I'll to the Officers; go you before
    And set an edge upon the Executioner.

Sup. Let me alone to grind.   *Exit.*

Ambi. Meete farewell.
    I am next now, I rise in that place
    Where thou'rt cut off; upon thy Neck, kind brother
    The falling of one head lifts up another. *Exit.*

      [SCENE II.]

 Enter with the Nobles Lussurioso *from pryson.*

Luss. My Lords, I am so much indebted to your loues
    For this O this deliuery.

1. *Nob.* Put our dueties, my Lord, unto the hopes that
    growe in you.

Luss. If ere I liue to be my selfe I'll thanke you.
    O liberty, thou sweete and heauenly Dame,
    But hell for pryson is too milde a name. *Exeunt.*

[SCENE III.]

Enter AMBITIOSO *and* SUPERUACUO *with officers.*

Amb. Officers, here's the Duke's signet, your firme warrant,
    Brings the command of present death along with it
    Unto our brother the Duke's sonne; we are sory
    That we are so unnaturally employ'd
    In such an unkinde office, fitter farre
    For enemies than brothers.

Super. But you know the Duke's command must be obey'd.

1. *Offi.* It must and shal, my Lord, this morning then,—
    So suddainely.

Amb. Aye alasse, poore good soule,
    Hee must breake fast betimes, the executioner
    Stands ready to put forth his cowardly valour.

2. *Offi.* Already.

Super. Already i'faith, O sir destruction hies
    And that is least Impudent soonest dyes.

1. *Offi.* Troth, you say true my Lord, we take our leaue
    Our Office shall be found, wee'll not delay
    The third part of a minute.

Amb. Therein you showe
    Your selves good men and upright. Officers
    Pray let him die as priuat as he may,
    Doe him that fauour, for the gaping people
    Will but trouble him at his prayers,
    And make him curse and sweare, and so die black.
    Will you be so far kind?

1. *Offi.* It shall be done my Lord.

Amb. Why we do thanke you, if we liue to be
    You shall haue a better office.

2. *Offi.* Your good Lordship.

Super. Commend us to the scaffold in our teares.

1. *Offi.* Wee'll weepe and doe your commendations.

                                          Exeunt.

Amb. Fine fooles in office. *Sup.* Things fall out so fit.

Ambi. So happily, come brother, ere next clock
>His head will be made serue a bigger block.
>>*Exeunt.*

SCENE IV.

Enter in pryson JUNIOR BROTHER

Juni. Keeper   *Keep.* My Lord.

Juni. No news lately from our brothers,
>Are they unmindfull of us?

Keep. My Lord a messenger came newly in,
>And brought this from 'em.

Juni. Nothing but paper comforts
I look'd for my deliuery before this
Had they beene worth their oths.—Prithee be
. from us.—
Now what say you forsooth, speake out I pray,
>Letter *Brother be of good cheere*

'Slud it begins like a whore with good cheere.
>*Thou shalt not be long a prisoner.*

Not sixe and thirty yeare like a banqrout I tninke so
>*We haue thought upon a deuice to get thee out by tricke*

By a tricke? Pox a' your tricke, an it be so long playing.

And so rest comforted be merry and expect it suddainely.

Be merry, hang merry, draw and quarter merry, I'll be mad

Is't not strange that a man should lie in a whole month for a woman? Well wee shall see how suddaine our brothers will bee in their promise. I must expect still a tricke. I shall not be long a prisoner? How now what newes?

Keep. Bad newes my Lord, I am discharg'd of you.

Juni. Slave call'st thou that bad newes? I thanke you brothers.

Keep. My Lord 'twill proue so, here come the officers
Into whose hands I must commit you.

Juni. Ha, Officers, what why?

1. *Offi.* You must pardon us, my Lord
Our Office must be sound; here is our warrant
The signet from the Duke, you must straight suffer.

Juni. Suffer! I'll suffer you to be gon. I'll suffer you

To come no more. What would you haue me
suffer?

2. *Offi.* My Lord, those words were better chang'd to
praiers,
The time's but briefe with you, prepare to die.

Juni. Sure tis not so.   3. *Offi.* It is too true my Lord.

Juni. I tell you 'tis not, for the Duke my father
Defer'd me till next sitting, and I looke
E'en euery minute, threescore times an houre,
For a release, a trick wrought by my brothers.

1. *Offi.* A trick my Lord? if you expect such comfort
Your hope's as fruitlesse as a barren woman.
Your brothers were the unhappy messengers,
That brought this powerfull token for your death.

Junior. My brothers? no, no.

2. *Offi.* 'Tis most true my Lord.

Junior. My brothers to bring a warrant for my death!
How strange this showes!

3. *Offi.* There's no delaying time.

Junior. Desire 'em hether—call 'em up—my brothers.
They shall deny it to your faces.

1. *Offi.* My Lord
>They're far ynough by this, at least, at Court
>And this most strickt command they left behinde
>'em
>When griefe swum in their eyes, they show'd like
>brothers
>Brim-full of heauy sorrow; but the Duke
>Must haue his pleasure. *Junior.* His pleasure?

1. *Offi.* These were their last words which my memory
>beares—

Commend us to the Scaffold in our teares.

Junior. Pox drye their teares. What should I do with
>teares?
>I hate 'em worse then any Cittizen's sonne
>Can hate salt water. Here came a letter now
>New-bleeding from their Pens, scarce stinted yet
>Would I'd beene torne in peeces when I tore it.
>Looke you, officious whoresons, words of comfort
>*Not long a Prisoner.*

1. *Offi.* It sayes true in that sir, for you must suffer pre-
>sently.

Junior. A villanous Duns upon the letter, knauish exposi-
>tion

Looke you then here sir : *Wee'll get thee out by a trick*—sayes hee.

2. *Offi.* That may hold too sir, for you know a trick is commonly foure Cardes, which was meant by us foure officers.

Junior. Worse and worse dealing.

1. *Offi.* The houre beckens us :
The heads-man waites; lift up your eyes to heauen.

Junior. I thanke you' faith, good pritty holsome counsell—
I should looke up to heauen as you sedd,
Whilst he behinde me cozens me of my head.
Aye that's the trick ! 3. *Offi.* You delay too long my Lord.

Junior. Stay, good Authoritie's Bastards. Since I must
Through Brothers' periurie dye, O let me venome
Their soules with curses ! 1. *Offi.* Come 'tis no time to curse.

Junior. Must I bleed then without respect of signe ? Well
My fault was sweet sport, which the world approues.
I dye for that which euery woman loues. *Exeunt.*

[SCENE V]

Enter VINDICI *with* HIPPOLITO *his brother.*

Vind. O sweete, delectable, rare, happy rauishing!

Hip. Why what's the matter brother?

Vind. O 'tis able
To make a man spring up and knock his for-head
Against yon siluar seeling.

Hip. Pre-thee tell mee
Why may I pertake with you? You vowde once
To giue me share to euery tragick thought.

Vind. Byth' Masse I thinke I did too.
Then I'll diuide it to thee. The old Duke
Thinking my outward shape and inward heart
Are cut out of one peice (for he that prates his
    secrets
His heart stands 'ath' side) hires me by price
To greete him with a Lady
In some fit place vaylde from the eyes a'th' Court,
Some darken'd blushlesse Angle that is guilty
Of his fore-fathers lusts and great-folkes riots,
To which I easily (to maintaine my shape)

      Consented and did wish his impudent grace
      To meete her here in this un-sunned lodge,
      Where-in 'tis night at noone, and here the rather,
      Because, unto the torturing of his soule,
      The Bastard and the Duchesse haue appoynted
      Their meeting too in this luxurious circle,
      Which most afflicting sight will kill his eyes
      Before we kill the rest of him.

Hip. 'Twill 'yfaith, most dreadfully digested
      I see not how you could haue mist me brother.

Vind. True, but the violence of my joy forgot it.

Hip. Aye, but where's that Lady now?

Vind. Oh at that word
      I'me lost againe. you cannot finde me yet
      I'me in a throng of happy Apprehensions.
      Hee's suted for a Lady. I haue tooke care
      For a delitious lip, a sparkling eye.
      You shall be witnesse brother.
      Be ready, stand with your hat off.   *Exit.*

Hip. Troth I wonder what Lady it should be.
      Yet 'tis no wonder now I thinke againe

To haue a Lady stoope to a Duke that stoopes
unto his men.
'Tis common to be common through the world
And there's more priuate common shadowing vices
Than those who are knowne both by their names
and prices.
Tis part of my alleagance to stand bare
To the Duke's Concubine,—and here she comes!

Re enter VINDICI *with the skull of his loue drest up in tires.*

Vind. Madame his grace will not be absent long.
Secret? Ne're doubt us Madame, 'twill be worth
Three veluet gownes to your Ladyship—knowne?
Few Ladies respect that disgrace a poore thin shell.
'Tis the best grace you haue to do it well
I'll saue your hand that labour, I'll unmaske you.

Hip. Why brother! brother!

Vind. Art thou beguild now? 'tut, a Lady can
At such all-hid beguile a wiser man.
Haue I not fitted the old surfetter
With a quaint piece of beauty? Age and bare bone
Are e'er allied in action, here's an eye
Able to tempt a great man——to serue God

A prety hanging lip that has forgot now to dissemble,

Me thinkes this mouth should make a swearer tremble,

A drunckard claspe his teeth and not undo 'em
To suffer wet damnation to run through 'em.
Here's a cheeke keepes her colour,—let the winde go whistle,

Spout Raine, we feare thee not—be hot or cold
All's one with us; and is not he absurd
Whose fortunes are upon their faces set
That feare no other God but winde and wet?

Hip. Brother y'aue spoke that right.
Is this the forme that liuing shone so bright?

Vind. The very same.
   · And now me-thinkes I could e'en chide my selfe
For doating on her beauty, tho' her death
Shall be reueng'd after no common action.
Does the Silke-worme expend her yellow labours
For thee? for thee does she undoe herselfe?
Are Lordships sold to maintaine Ladyships
For the poore benefit of a bewitching minute?
Why does yon fellow falsify hie-waies

And put his life betweene the Judge's lippes?
To refine such a thing, keepes horse and men
To beate their valours for her?
Surely wee're all mad people, and they
Whome we thinke are, are not, we mistake those
'Tis we are mad in scence, they but in clothes.

Hip. Faith and in clothes too we—giue us our due.

Vind. Does euery proud and selfe-affecting Dame
Camphire her face for this, and grieue her Maker
In sinfull baths of milke?—when many an infant starues
For her superfluous out-side, all for this?
Who now bids twenty pound a night, prepares
Musick, perfumes, and sweete-meates? All are husht.
Thou maist lie chast now! It were fine me-thinkes
To haue thee seene at Reuells, forgetfull feasts
And uncleane Brothells! sure 'twould fright the sinner
And make him a good coward; put a Reueller
Out of his Antick amble,
And cloye an Epicure with empty dishes!
Here might a scornefull and ambitious woman

Looke through and through her selfe,——see
  Ladies, with false formes
You deceiue men, but cannot deceiue wormes.
Now to my tragick business. Looke you brother
I haue not fashion'd this onely for show
And uselesse property, no, it shall beare a part
E'ene in its owne Reuenge. This very skull,
Whose Mistris the Duke poysonéd, with this drug
The mortall curse of the earth shall be reuengd
In the like straine, and kisse his lippes to death.
As much as the dumbe thing can, he shall feele,
What fayles in poyson wee'l supply in steele.

Hip. Brother, I do applaud thy constant vengeance,
  The quaintnesse of thy malice aboue thought.

Vind. So 'tis layde on. Now come and welcome Duke,
  I haue her for thee. I protest it, brother,
  Me thinkes she makes almost as faire a fine
  As some old gentlewoman in a Periwig.
  Hide thy face now for shame. Thou hadst neede
    haue a Maske now;
  'Tis vaine when beauty flowes, but when it fleetes
  This would become graues better than the streetes.

Hip. You haue my voice in that; harke, the Duke's come.

Vind. Peace, let's obserue what company he brings
And how he does absent 'em; for you knowe
Hee'll wish all priuate, brother fall you back a little
With the bony Lady.   *Hip.* That I will.

Vind. So, so; now nine years vengeance crowde into a minute!

Duke. You shall haue leaue to leaue us, with this charge
Upon your liues, if we be mist by th' Duchesse,
Or any of the Nobles, to giue out
We're priuately rid forth.   *Vind.* Oh happinesse!

Duke. With some few honorable gentlemen you may say,—
You may name those that are away from Court.

Gentle. Your will and pleasure shall be done, my Lord.

Vind. Priuately rid forth!
He striues to make sure worke on't,—your good grace

Duke. Piato, well done; hast brought her? What Lady is't?

Vind. Faith my Lord a Country Lady, a little bashfull

at first, as most of them are, but after the first kisse, my Lord, the worst is past with them; your grace knowes now what you haue to doo— she's some-what a graue looke with her— but——

Duke. I loue that best, conduct her.

Vind. Haue at all.

Duke. In grauest lookes the Greatest faultes seeme lesse
Giue me that sin that's rob'd in Holines.

Vind. Back with the Torch: brother raise the perfumes.

Duke. How sweete can a Duke breathe! age has no fault
Pleasure should meete in a perfumed mist.
Lady, sweetly encountred. I came from Court
I must bee bould with you. Oh! what's this! oh!

Vind. Royall villaine! white diuill! *Duke.* Oh!

Vind. Brother place the torch here, that his affrighted eye-balls
May start into those hollowes. Duke, dost knowe
Yon dreadfull vizard? view it well, 'tis the skull
Of Gloriana whom thou poysonedst last.

Duke. Oh, 't'as poysoned me!

Vind. Didst not know that till now?

Duke. What are you two?

Vind. Villaines all three,—the very ragged bone
    Has beene sufficiently reueng'd.

Duke. Oh Hippolito, call treason.

Hip. Yes my good Lord, treason! treason! treason!
                              Stamping on him.

Duke. Then I'me betrayde.

Vind. Alasse poore Lecher in the hands of knaues!
    A slauish Duke is baser then his slaues.

Duke. My teeth are eaten out.   *Vind.* Hadst any left?

Hip. I thinke but few.

Vind. Then those that did eate are eaten.   *Duke.* O my
    tongue!

Vind. Your tongue! 'Twill teach you to kisse closer,
    Not like a slobbering Dutchman; you haue eyes
      still
    Looke monster what a Lady hast thou made me
    My once bethrothed wife.

Duke. Is it thou villaine? nay then——

Vind. 'Tis I, 'tis Vindici, 'tis I.

Hip. And let this comfort thee. Our Lord and Father

Fell sick upon the infection of thy frownes
And dyed in sadnesse ; be that thy hope of life.
Duke. Oh !

Vind. He had his tong, yet greefe made him die speechlesse.
Puh, tis but early yet ! now I'll begin
To stick thy soule with Ulcers : I will make
Thy spirit grieuous sore, it shall not rest
But like some pestilent man tosse in thy brest.
Marke me duke
Thou'rt a renowned, high, and mighty Cuckold.

Duke. Oh !

Vind. Thy Bastard, thy bastard rides a hunting in thy browe.

Duke. Millions of deaths !

Vind. Nay to afflict thee more
Here in this lodge they meete for damned clips,
Those eyes shall see the incest of their lips.

Duke. Is there a hell besides this, villaines ?   *Vind.* Villaine
Nay heauen is just, scornes are the hire of scornes
I nere knew yet Adulterer without hornes.

Hip. Once ere they dye 'tis quitted.

Vind. Harke the musicke.
Their banquet is preparde; they're coming.

Duke. Oh kill me not with that sight!

Vind. Thou shalt not lose that sight for all thy Duke-doome.

Duke. Traytors! murderers!

Vind. What is not thy tongue eaten out yet?
Then wee'll inuent a silence; brother stifle the Torch.

Duke. Treason! murther!

Vind. Nay faith, wee'll haue you husht now with thy dagger;
Naile downe his tongue, and mine shall keepe possession
About his heart, if he but gaspe hee dyes.
We dread not death to quittance injuries.
Brother if he but winck, not brooking the foule object,
Let our two other hands teare up his lids,
And make his eyes like Comets shine through bloud.

When the bad bleedes, then is the Tragedie good.

Hip. Whist, brother, the musick's at our eare! they come.

Enter the Bastard meeting the Duchesse.

Spu. Had not that kisse a taste of sinne, 'twere sweete.

Dutch. Why there's no pleasure sweet but it is sinfull.

Spu. True, such a bitter sweetnesse fate has giuen
Best side to us is the worst side to heauen.

Dutch. Push! come, 'tis the old Duke thy doubtfull Father.
The thought of him rubs heauen in thy way,
But I protest, by yonder waxen fire
Forget him, or I'll poyson him.

Spu. Madam, you urge a thought which nere had life,
So deadly doe I loath him for my birth,
That if hee tooke mee haspt within his bed
I would adde murther to adultery
And with my sword giue up his yeares to death.

Dutch. Why now thou'rt sociable, let's in and feast.
Lowd'st Musick sound; pleasure is Banquet's guest. *Exeunt.*

Duke. I cannot brooke——*Vind.* The Brooke is turned
    to bloud.
Hip. Thanks to lowd Musick. *Vind.* 'Twas our friend
    indeed.
    'Tis state in Musicke for a Duke to bleed.
    The Duke-dome wants a head, tho' yet unknowne.
    As fast as they peepe up, lets cut 'em downe.
                                 Exeunt.

[SCENE VI]

Enter the Dutchesse two sonnes, AMBITIOSO *and* SUPERU-
ACUO.

Amb. Was not his execution rarely plotted?
    We are the Duke's sonnes now.
Super. Aye, you may thanke my policie for that.
Amb. Your policie for what?
Super. Why was't not my inuention brother
    To slip the Judges, and in lesser compasse
    Did I not draw the modell of his death
    Aduizing you to suddaine officers
    And e'en extemporall execution?
Amb. Heart, 'twas a thing I thought on too.

Super. You thought on't too! sfoote slander not your
    thoughts
  With glorious untruth. I know 'twas from you.

Amb. Sir, I say 'twas in my head.

Super. Aye, like your braines then
  Nere to come out as long as you liu'd.

Amb. You'd haue the honor on't forsooth that your wit
  Lead him to the scaffold.

Super. Since it is my due
  I'll publish't, but I'll ha't in spite of you.

Amb. Me thinkes y'are much too bould, you should a
    little
  Remember us brother next to be honest Duke.

Super. Aye, it shall be as easie for you to be Duke
  As to be honest, and that's neuer i'faith.

Amb. Well, cold he is by this time, and because
  Wee're both ambitious be it our amity
  And let the glory be shar'd equally. *Super.* I am
    content to that.

Amb. This night our younger brother shall out of prison;
  I haue a trick. *Super.* A trick? pre-thee what is't?

Amb. Wee'll get him out by a wile. *Super.* Pre-thee what wile?

Amb. No sir you shall not know it till't be done
For then you'd sweare 'twere yours.

Super. How now? whats he? *Amb.* One of the officers.

Super. Desired newes! *Amb.* How now my friend?

Off. My Lords, under your pardon I am allotted
To that desertlesse office, to present you
With the yet bleeding head. *Super.* Ha, ha! excellent!

Amb. All's sure our owne. Brother, canst weepe thinkst thou?
'Twould grace our Flattery much; thinke of some Dame
'Twill teach thee to dissemble.

Super. I haue thought. Now for your selfe.

Amb. Our sorrowes are so fluent
Our eyes ore-flow our tongs, words spoke in teares
Are like the murmures of the waters, the sound
Is lowdly heard, but cannot be distinguisht.

Super. How dyed he pray? *Off.* O full of rage and
    spleene.

Super. He dyed most valiantly then : we're glad to heare
    it.

Off. We could not woe him once to pray.

Amb. He showd himselfe a Gentleman in that : giue
    him his due.

Off. But in the stead of prayer he drew forth oaths.

Super. Then did hee pray, deere heart,
    Although you understood him not.

Off. My Lords,
    E'en at his last, with pardon bee it spoake,
    Hee curst you both.

Super. Hee curst us ? 'lasse good soule !

Amb. It was not in our powers, but the Dukes pleasure.
    Finely dissembled at both-sides.   Sweete fate !
    O happy opportunitie !   *Enter* LUSSURIOSO.

Luss. Now my Lords.   *Both.* Oh !——

Luss. Why doe you shunne mee Brothers ?
    You may come neerer now
    The sauor of the prison has for-sooke mee.

I thanke such kinde Lords as your selues I'm free.

Amb. Aliue! *Super.* In health!

Amb. Releas'd?
We were both e'en amazd with joy to see it.

Luss. I am much to thanke you.

Super. Faith, we spar'd no tong unto my Lord the Duke.

Amb. I know your deliuery brother
Had not beene halfe so sudden but for us.

Super. O how we pleaded! *Luss.* Most deseruing brothers!
In my best studies I will thinke of it. *Exit* Luss.

Amb. O death and vengeance! *Super.* Hell and torments!

Amb. Slaue, cam'st thou to delude us? *Off.* Delude you my Lords?

Super. Aye villaine, where's this head now?

Off. Why heere, my Lord.
Just after his deliuery you both came

With warrant from the Duke to be-head your brother.

Amb. Aye, our brother—the Duke's sonne.

Off. The Duke's sonne, my Lord, had his release before you came.

Amb. Whose head's that then?

Off. His whom you left command for—your owne brother's!

Amb. Our brother's?   O furies!

Super. Plagues!   *Amb.* Confusions!

Super. Darkenesse!   *Amb.* Diuills!

Super. Fell it out so accursedly?   *Amb.* So damnedly?

Super. Villaine I'll braine thee with it.   *Off.* O my good Lord!

Super. The Diuill ouer-take thee!   *Amb.* O fatall!

Super. O prodigious to our blouds!   *Amb.* Did we dissemble?

Super. Did we make our teares woemen for thee?

Amb. Laugh and rejoyce for thee?

Super. Bring warrant for thy death?

Amb. Mock off thy head?

Super. You had a trick! You had a wile forsooth!

Amb. A murren meete 'em! there's none of these wiles that euer come to good. I see now there is nothing sure in mortalitie but mortalitie. Well no more words. Shalt be reuengd i'faith.
Come, throw off clouds now brother, thinke of vengeance
And deeper settled hate. Sirrah, sit fast.
Wee'll pull downe all, but thou shalt downe at last. *Exeunt.*

ACT. 4. SCEN. I.

Enter LUSSURIOSO *with* HIPPOLITO.

Luss. Hippolito ! *Hip.* My Lord,
Has your good Lordship ought to command me in ?

Luss. I pre-thee leaue us.

Hip. How's this ? come—and leaue us ! *Luss.* Hippolito !

Hip. Your honor, I stand ready for any dutious emploiment.

Luss. 'Heart, what mak'st thou here ?

Hip. A pritty Lordly humor !
He bids me to bee present, to depart !
Something has stung his honor.

Luss. Bee neerer, draw neerer.
Y'are not so good me-thinkes. I'me angry with you.

Hip. With me my Lord ? I'me angry with my selfe for't.

Luss. You did preferre a goodly fellow to me.

'Twas wittily elected, 'twas, I thought
He'd beene a villaine, and he prooues a Knaue!
To mee a Knaue!

Hip. I chose him for the best, my Lord.
'Tis much my sorrow if neglect in him
Breed discontent in you.

Luss. Neglect! 'Twas Will (Judge of it)
Firmely to tell of an incredible Act,
Not to be thought, lesse to be spoken of,
'Twixt my Step-mother and the Bastard—Oh!
Incestuous sweetes betweene 'em.

Hip. Fye, my Lord!

Luss. I, in kinde loyaltie to my father's fore-head,
Made this a desperate arme, and in that furie
Committed treason on the lawfull bed,
And with my sword e'en ras'd my father's bosome,
For which I was within a stroake of death.

Hip. Alack, I'me sorry. 'Sfoote, just upon the stroake.
[Aside]
Jars in my brother. 'Twill be villainous Musick!

Vind. My honored Lord! *Enter* VINDICI.

Luss. Away, pre-thee forsake us! Hereafter wee'll not know thee.

Vind. Not know me, my Lord? Your Lordship cannot choose.

Luss. Begon, I say! Thou art a false knaue.

Vind. Why the easier to be knowne, my Lord!

Luss. Tush, I shall prooue too bitter; with a word
Make thee a perpetuall prisoner,
And laye this yron-age upon thee.

Vind. Mum,
—For there's a doome would make a woman dumb.
Missing the bastard, next him the winde's come about.
Now 'tis my brother's turne to stay, mine to goe out.

Luss. 'He's greatly moou'd me.   *Exit* VIND.

    Hip. Much to blame, i' faith!

Luss. But I'll recouer——to his ruine. 'Twas told me lately,
I know not whether falslie, that you'd a brother.

Hip. Who? I? Yes, my good Lord, I haue a brother.

Luss. How chance the Court neere saw him? Of what
nature?

How does he apply his houres?

Hip. Faith, to curse Fates
Who, as he thinkes, ordain'd him to be poore.
'Keepes at home full of want and discontent.

Luss. There's hope in him; for discontent and want
Is the best clay to mould a villaine of.
Hippolito, wish him to repaire to us.
If there be ought in him to please our bloud
For thy sake wee'll aduance him, and build faire
His meanest fortunes; for it is in us
To reare up Towers from cottages.

Hip. It is so, my Lord. He will attend your honour;—
But hee's a man in whom much melancholy dwels.

Luss. Why, the better! Bring him to Court.

Hip. With willingnesse and speed.
Whom he cast off e'en now, must now succeed.
Brother, disguise must off.
In thine owne shape now I'll prefer thee to him.
How strangely does himselfe worke to undo him!
Exit.

Luss. This fellow will come fitly; he shall kill
That other slaue that did abuse my spleene
And made it swell to Treason. I haue put
Much of my heart into him; he must dye.
He that knowes great mens' secrets and proues slight,
That man nere liues to see his Beard turne white.
Aye, he shall speede him. I'll employ thee, brother.
Slaues are but Nayles to driue out one another!
Hee being of black condition, sutable
To want and ill content, hope of preferment
Will grinde him to an Edge. *The Nobles enter.*

1. *Noble.* Good dayes unto your honour!

Luss. My kinde Lords, I do return the like.

2. *Noble.* Sawe you my Lord the Duke?

Luss. My Lord and Father, is he from Court?

1. *Noble.* Hee's sure from Court.
But where, which way his pleasure tooke we know not;
Nor can wee heare on't.

Luss. Here come those should tell.
Sawe you my Lord and Father?

3. *Noble.* Not since two houres before noone, my Lord;
 And then he priuately ridde forth.

Luss. Oh hee's rode forth!

1. *Noble.* 'Twas wondrous priuately.

2. *Noble.* There's none i'th Court had any knowledge on't.

Luss. His grace is old and sudden. 'Tis no treason
 To say the Duke my Father has a humor,
 Or such a Toye about him. What in us
 Would appeare light, in him seemes vertuous.

3. *Noble.* 'Tis Oracle, my Lord. *Exeunt.*

[SCENE II.]

Enter VINDICI *and* HIPPOLITO. VIND. *out of his disguise.*

Hip. So, so! All's as it should be. Y'are your selfe.

Vind. How that great villaine puts me to my shifts!

Hip. Hee that did lately in disguize reject thee
 Shall, now thou art thy selfe, as much respect thee.

Vind. 'Twill be the quainter fallacie. But, brother,
 'Sfoote, what use will hee put me to now, think'st
 thou?

Hip. Nay, you must pardon me in that; I know not.

He's some employment for you, but what 'tis
Hee and his Secretary the Diuell knowes best.

Vind. Well, I must suite my toung to his desires
What colour soere they be; hoping at last
To pile up all my wishes on his brest.

Hip. Faith, Brother, he himselfe showes the way!

Vind. Now the Duke is dead, the realme is clad in claye,
His death being not yet knowne, under his name
The people still are gouern'd. Well, thou his sonne
Art not long-liu'd: thou shalt not joy his death.
To kill thee then I should most honour thee;
For 'twould stand firme in euery man's beliefe
Thou'dst a kinde child and onely dye'dst with griefe.

Hip. You fetch about well, but let's talke in present.
How will you appeare in fashion different,
As well as in apparrell, to make all things possible?
If you be but once tript wee fall for euer.
It is not the least pollicie to bee doubtfull:
You must change tongue—familiar was your first.

Vind. Why, I'll beare me in some straine of melancholie

And string my selfe with heauy-sounding Wyre,
Like such an Instrument that speakes
Merry things sadly.

Hip. Then 'tis as I meant.

. I gaue you out at first in discontent.

Vind. I'll turne my selfe, and then——

Hip. 'Sfoote, here he comes! Hast thought uppon't?

Vind. Salute him: feare not me. *Luss.* Hippolito!

Hip. Your Lordship. *Luss.* What's he yonder?

Hip. 'Tis Vindici, my discontented Brother,
Whom, 'cording to your will, I haue brought to
Court.

Luss. Is that thy brother? beshrew me, a good
presence!
I wonder 'has beene from the Court so long!
Come neerer.

Hip. Brother, Lord Lussurioso, the Duke's sonne.

Luss. Be more neere to us: welcome; neerer yet.

Vind. How don you? god you god den!
        Snatches off his hat and makes legs to him.

Luss. We thanke thee.

How strangely such a coarse-homely salute
Showes in the Pallace, where we greete in fire
Nimble and desperate tongues ! Should we name
God in a salutation, 'twould neere be stood on't,—
 Heauen ! Tell me] what has made thee so
 melancholy?

Vind. Why, going to Law !

Luss. Why, will that make a man mellancholy ?

Vind. Yes, to looke long vpon inck and black buckrom.
 I went mee to law in *Anno Quadragesimo
 secundo,* and I waded out of it *Anno sexagesimo
 tertio.*

Luss. What, three and twenty years in law ?

Vind. I haue knowne those that haue beene fiue and
 fifty, and all about Pullin and Pigges.

Luss. Nay it bee possible such men should breathe
 To vex the Tearmes so much ?

Vind. 'Tis foode to some, my Lord. There are olde men
 at the present that are so poysoned with the
 affectation of law-words (hauing had many suites
 canvast) that their common talke is nothing but
 Barbery Lattin : they cannot so much as pray,

but in law, that their sinnes may be remou'd with a writ of Error, and their soules fecht up to heauen with a fafarara.

It seemes most strange to me.
Yet all the world meetes round in the same bent;
Where the heart's set there goes the tongues consent.
How dost apply thy studies, fellow?

Vind. Study? Why to thinke how a great rich man lies a dying, and a poore Cobler toales the bell for him. How he cannot depart the world and see the great chest stand before him, when he lies speechlesse how hee will point you readily to all the boxes; and when hee is past all memory, as the gosseps gesse, then thinkes hee of forfettures and obligations. Nay, when to all mens' hearings he whurles and rottes in the throate hee's busie threat'ning his poore Tennants. And this would last me now some seauen yeares thinking, or there abouts; but I haue a Conceit a'comming in picture upon this. I drawe it my selfe, which i'faith, la! I'll present to your honor.

You shall not chose but like it, for your Lordship
Shall giue me nothing for it.

Luss. Nay, you misstake me then,
For I am publisht bountifull enough.
Let's taste of your conceit.

Vind. In picture, my Lord? *Luss.* Aye, in picture.

Vind. Marry, this it is—— *A usuring Father to be boyling in hell, and his sonne and Heire with a Whore dancing ouer him.*

Hip. Has't par'd him to the quicke. [Aside]

Luss. The conceit's pritty i'faith;
But tak't upon my life 'twill nere be likt.

Vind. No? Why I'm sure the whore will be likt well enough.

Hip: Aye, if she were out a'th' picture, hee'd like her then himselfe.

Vind. And as for the sonne and heire,—he shall be an eyesore to no young Reuellers, for he shall bee drawne in cloth of gold breeches.

Luss. And thou hast put my meaning in the pockets,
And canst not draw that out. My thought was this:—

To see the picture of a usuring father
Boyling in hell ; our richmen would nere like it.

Vind. O true ! I cry you heartily mercy ! I know the
reason, for some of 'em had rather be damn'd
indeed, then damn'd in colours.

Luss. A parlous melancholy ! Has wit enough
To murder any man, and I'll giue him meanes.
I thinke thou art ill-monied.

Vind. Money ? ho, ho !
'Tas beene my want so long 'tis now my scoffe.
I'ue ene forgot what colour siluer's of.

Luss. It hits as I could wish. *Vind.* I get good cloths
Of those that dread my humour, and for table-
roome
I feed on those that cannot be rid of me.

Luss. Somewhat to set thee up withall.

Vind. O mine eyes ! *Luss.* How now, man ?

Vind. Almost strucke blind.
This bright unusuall shine to me seemes proud :
I dare not looke till the sunne be in a cloud.

Luss. I thinke I shall affect his melancholy.

How are they now? *Vind.* The better for your
asking.

Luss. You shall be better yet, if you but fasten
Truly on my intent. Now y'are both present
I will unbrace such a closse priuate villayne
Unto your vengfull swords, the like nere heard of,
Who hath disgrac'd you much and injur'd us.

Hip. Disgraced us, my Lord?

Luss. Aye, Hippolito.
I kept it here till now, that both your angers
Might meete him at once.

Vind. I'm couetous
To know the villayne.

Luss. You know him; that slaue Pandar,
Piato, whome we threatened last
With irons in perpetuall prisonment.

Vind. All this is I! *Hip.* Is't he, my Lord?

Luss. I'll tell you. You first prefer'd him to me.

Vind. Did you, brother? *Hip.* I did indeed

Luss. And the ungreatfull villayne
To quit that kindnes strongly wrought with me—

  Being as you see a likely man for pleasure—
  With jewels to corrupt your virgin sister!

Hip. O villaine!   *Vind.* He shall surely die that did it.

Luss. I, far from thinking any Virgin harme,
  Especially knowing her to be as chaste
  As that part which scarce suffers to be toucht—
  Th' eye—would not endure him.

Vind. Would you not, my Lord?
  'Twas wondrous honorably donne!

Luss. But with some fine frownes kept him out.

Vind. Out, slaue!

Luss. What did me he but in reuenge of that
  Went of his owne free will to make infirme
  Your sister's honor, whome I honor with my soule
  For chaste respect; and not preuayling there
  (As 'twas but desperate folly to attempt it)
  In meere spleene, by the way, way-laies your
   mother,
  Whose honor being a coward as it seemes
  Yeelded by little force.   *Vind.* Coward indeed!

Luss. He proud of their aduantage, as he thought,

   Brought me these newes for happy ; but I—
   Heauen forgiue mee for't———

Vind. What did your honour ?

Luss. In rage pusht him from mee,
   Trampled beneath his throate, spurn'd him, and
    bruiz'd.
   Indeed I was too cruell, to say troth.

Hip. Most Nobly managde !

Vind. Has not heauen an eare ? Is all the lightning
   wasted ?   [Aside]

Luss. If I now were so impatient in a modest cause,
   What should you be ?

Vind. Full mad ! He shall not liue
   To see the Moone change.

Luss. He's about the Pallace.
   Hippolito intice him this way, that thy brother
   May take full marke of him.

Hip. 'Heart, that shall not neede, my Lord,
   I can direct him so far.

Luss. Yet for my hate's sake
   Go winde him this way. I'll see him bleede my
    selfe.

Hip. What now, brother?

Vind. Nay, e'en what you will: y'are put to it, brother!

Hip. An impossible taske, I'll sweare,   [Aside]
To bring him hither that's already here.

                                    Exit HIPPO.

Luss. Thy name? I haue forgot it.   *Vind.* Vindici, my Lord.

Luss. 'Tis a good name that.   *Vind.* Aye, a Reuenger.

Luss. It does betoken courage;—thou shouldst be valiant
And kill thine enemies.   *Vind.* That's my hope, my Lord.

Luss. This slaue is one.   *Vind.* I'll doome him.

Luss. Then I'll praise thee.
Do thou obserue me best and I'll best raise thee.

Vind. Indeed I thanke you.   *Re-enter Hip.*

Luss. Now Hippolito, where's the slaue Pandar?

Hip. Your good Lordship
Would haue a loathsome sight of him, much offensiue!

Hee's not in case now to be seene, my Lord.
The worst of all the deadly sinnes is in him —
That beggerly damnation—drunkennesse.

Luss. Then he's a double-slaue!

Vind. 'Twas well conuaide upon a suddaine wit.
[Aside]

Luss. What, are you both
Firmely resolued? I'll see him dead my selfe.

Vind. Or else let not us liue.

Luss. You may direct your brother to take note of him.

Hip. I shall.

Luss. Rise but in this, and you shall neuer fall.

Vind. Your honour's Vassayles.

Luss. This was wisely carried. [Aside]
Deepe policie in us makes fooles of such.
Then must a slaue die when he knowes too much.
Exit Luss.

Vind. O thou almighty patience! 'tis my wonder
That such a fellow, impudent and wicked,
Should not be clouen as he stood,
Or with a secret winde burst open.

Is there no thunder left? or is't kept up
In stock for heauier vengeance?   There it goes!
[Thunder]

Hip. Brother, we lose our selues.

Vind. But I haue found it.
'Twill hold, 'tis sure; thankes, thankes to any spirit
That mingled it 'mongst my inuentions.

Hip. What is't?

Vind. 'Tis sound and good.   Thou shalt partake it,—
I'm hir'd to kill my selfe—   *Hip.* True.

Vind. Pree-thee marke it,—
And the old Duke being dead, but not conuaide—
For he's already mist too, and you know
Murder will peepe out of the closest huske——

Hip. Most true!

Vind. What say you then to this deuice,
If we drest up the body of the Duke?

Hip. In that disguise of yours?

Vind. Y'are quick; y'aue reacht it.

Hip. I like it wonderously.

Vind. And being in drinck, as you haue publisht him,
> To lean him on his elbowe, as if sleepe had caught him,
Which claimes most interest in such sluggy men.

Hip. Good yet, but here's a doubt;
> We, thought by th' Duke's sonne to kill that pandar,
Shall, when he is knowne, be thought to kill the Duke.

Vind. Neither, O thankes. it is substantiall
For that disguize being on him which I wore
It will be thought I, which he calls the Pandar, did kil the Duke and fled away in his apparell, leauing him so disguiz'd to auoide swift pursuite. *Hip.* Firmer and firmer!

Vind. Nay, doubt not 'tis in graine: I warrant it hold collour

Hip. Let's about it.

Vind. But by the way too, now I thinke on't, brother,
Let's conjure that base diuill out of our Mother.
Exeunt.

[SCENE III.]

Enter the Duches arme in arme with the Bastard; he seemeth lasciuiously. After them, Enter SUPERUACUO *running with a rapier; his Brother stops him.*

Spu. Madam, unlock your selfe. Should it be seene,
    Your arme would be suspected.

Duch. Who is't that dares suspect or this or these?
    May not we deale our fauors where we please?

Spu. I'm confident you may.   *Exeunt.*

Amb. 'Sfoot, brother, hold.

Sup. Wouldst let the Bastard shame us?

Amb. Hold, hold, brother! There's fitter time then
    now.

Sup. Now, when I see it. *Amb.* 'Tis too much seene
    already.

Sup. Seene and knowne!
    The Nobler she's, the baser is shee growne.

Amb. If she were bent lasciuiously—the fault
    Of mighty women that sleepe soft—O death!

Must she needes chuse such an vnequall sinner
To make all worse?

Sup. A Bastard! the Dukes Bastard! Shame heapt on
shame!

Amb. O our disgrace!
Most women haue small waste the world through-
out,
But their desires are thousand miles about.

Sup. Come, stay not here: let's after and preuent;
Or els they'll sinne faster then weele repent.

Exeunt.

[SCENE IV.]

Enter VINDICI *and* HIPPOLITO, *bringing out their Mother,
one by one shoulder, and the other by the other, with
daggers in their hands.*

Vindi. O thou for whom no name is bad ynough!

Moth. What meane my sonnes? What will you murder
me?

Vind. Wicked, unnaturall Parent!

Hip. Feend of women!

Moth. Oh! are sonnes turn'd monsters? Helpe!

Vind. In vaine.

Moth. Are you so barbarous to set Iron nipples
    Upon the breast that gaue you suck?

Vind. That breast
    Is turn'd to Quarled poyson.

Moth. Cut not your daies for't! Am not I your mother?

Vind. Thou dost usurpe that title now by fraud,
    For in that shell of mother breeds a bawde.

Moth. A bawde? O name far loathsomer than hell!

Hip. It should be so, knew'st thou thy Office well.

Moth. I hate it.

Vind. Ah, is't possible, thou onely? You powers on hie
    That women should dissemble when they die!

Moth. Dissemble?

Vind. Did not the Duke's sonne direct
    A fellow, of the world's condition, hither,
    That did corrupt all that was good in thee,
    Made thee unciuilly forget thy selfe,
    And worke our sister to his lust?

Moth. Who I?

>   That had beene monstrous! I defie that man
>   For any such intent. None liues so pure,
>   But shall be soil'd with slander. Good sonne,
>   Beleiue it not.

Vind. Oh, I'm in doubt
        Whether I'm my selfe or no.
        Stay, let me looke agen upon this face.—
        Who shall be sau'd when mothers haue no grace?

Hip. 'Twould make one halfe dispaire.

Vind. I was the man.
        Defie me now! let's see! do't modestly!

Moth. O hell unto my soule!

Vind. In that disguize I, sent from the Duke's sonne,
        Tryed you, and found you base mettell,
        As any villaine might haue done.

Moth. O no!
        No tongue but yours could haue bewitcht me so.

Vind. O nimble in damnation, quick in tune!
        There is no diuill could strike fire so soone.
        I am confuted in a word.

Moth. O sonnes, forgiue me! To my selfe I'll proue
more true.
You that should honor me, I kneele to you.

Vind. A mother to giue ayme to her owne daughter!

Hip. True, brother, how far beyond nature to't!
Tho' many Mothers do't.

Vind. Nay, an you draw teares once, go you to bed.
Wee will make iron blush, and change to red.
Brother, it raines; 'twill spoile your dagger, house
it.

Hip. 'Tis done.

Vind. Y'faith 'tis a sweete shower: it does much good.
The fruitfull grounds and meadowes of her soule
Have beene long dry. Powre downe, thou blessed
dew!
Rise Mother; troth, this shower has made you
higher.

Moth. O you heauens, take this infectious spot out of my
soule!
I'll rince it in seauen waters of mine eyes.
Make my teares salt ynough to taste of grace.

    To weepe is to our sexe naturally giuen ;
    But to weepe truely, that's a gift from heauen !

Vind. Nay, I'll kisse you now ; kisse her, brother.
    Let's marry her to our soules wherein's no lust,
    And honorably loue her. *Hip.* Let it be.

Vind. For honest women are so seld and rare,
    'Tis good to cherish those poore few that are.
    Oh you of easie waxe, do but imagine,
    Now the disease has left you, how leprously
    That Office would haue cling'd unto your forehead !
    All mothers that had any gracefull hue
    Would haue worne maskes, to hide their face at
     you.
    It would haue growne to this——at your foule
     name
    Greene-collour'd maides would haue turn'd red
     with shame !

Hip. And then our sister full of hire and bassenesse !

Vind. There had beene boyling lead again !
    Duke's sonne's great Concubine !
    A drab of State, a cloath, a siluer slut !
    To haue her traine borne up, and her soule traile
     i'th' durt—Great !—

Hip. Too miserably great ; rich, to be eternally wicked !

Vind. O common madnesse !
Aske but the thriuing'st harlot in cold bloud ;
Shee'd giue the world to make her honour good.
Perhaps you'll say,—but onely to th' Duke's sonne,
In priuate ; why, shee first begins with one
Who afterward to thousand prooues a whore.
Breake ice in once place, it will crack in more.

Moth. Most certainly applyed !

Hip. Oh Brother, you forget our businesse !

Vind. And well remembred ! Joye's a subtill elfe.
I thinke man's happiest when he forgets himselfe.
Farewell, once dryed, now holy-watred Meade !
Our hearts weare Feathers that before wore Lead.

Moth. I'll giue you this,—that one I neuer knew
Plead better for and 'gainst the Diuill then you.

Vind. You make me proud on't.

Hip. Commend us in all vertue to our Sister.

Vind. Aye, for the loue of heauen, to that true maide.

Moth. With my best words.

Vind. Why, that was motherly said !   *Exeunt.*

Moth. I wonder now what fury did transport me!
       I feel good thoughts begin to settle in me.
       Oh, with what fore-head can I looke on her,
       Whose honor I'ue so impiouslie beset!
       And here shee comes.   *Enter Castiza.*

Cast. Now, mother, you haue wrought with me so strongly,'
       That what for my aduancement, as to calme
       The trouble of your tongue, I am content——

Moth. Content? to what?

Cast. To do as you haue wisht me :—
       To prostitute my brest to the Duke's sonne,
       And put my selfe to common Usury.

Moth. I hope you will not so.

Cast. Hope you I will not?
       That's not the hope you looke to be saued in.

Moth. Truth, but it is.

Cast. Do not deceiue your selfe.
       I am, as you, e'en out of Marble wrought.
       What would you now? are yee not pleasde yet with me?

>   You shall not wish me to be more lasciuious
>   Then I intend to be. *Moth.* Strike not me cold.

Cast. How often haue you charg'd me on your blessing
>   To be a cursed woman! When you knew
>   Your blessing had no force to make me lewd,
>   You laide your curse upon me—that did more,—
>   The mother's curse is heauy; where that fights,
>   Sonnes set in storme and daughters lose their lights.

Moth. Good childe, deare maide, if there be any sparke
>   Of heauenly intellectuall fire within thee,
>   O let my breath reuiue it to a flame!
>   Put not all out with woman's wilfull follies.
>   I am recouer'd of that foule disease
>   That haunts too many mothers. Kinde, forgiue me;
>   Make me not sick in health! If then
>   My words preuailde when they were wickednesse,
>   How much more now when they are just and good!

Cast. I wonder what you meane! Are not you she
>   For whose infect perswasions I could scarce

Kneele out my prayers, and had much adoo,
In three houres reading, to untwist so much
Of the black serpent as you wound about me?

Moth. 'Tis unfruitfull, held tedious to repeate what's past.
I'm now your present Mother. *Cast.* Tush, now 'tis too late!

Moth. Bethinke agen. Thou know'st not what thou say'st.

Cast. No? Deny aduancement? treasure? the Dukes sonne?

Moth. O see! I spoke those words, and now they poyson me.
What will the deed do then?
Aduancement,—True! as high as shame can pitch.
For Treasure, who ere knew a harlot rich?
Or could build by the purchase of her sinne
An hospitall to keepe their bastards in?
The Duke's sonne!
Oh, when woemen are yong Courtiers they are sure to be old beggars!
To know the miseries most harlots taste
Thou'dst wish thy selfe unborne when thou art unchast.

Cast. O mother, let me twine about your necke,
    And kisse you till my soule melt on your lips!
    I did but this to trie you. *Moth.* O speake truth!

Cast. Indeed I did not; for no tong has force
    To alter me from honest.
    If maydens would, men's words could haue no power.
    A vergin's honor is a christall Tower,
    Which, being weake, is guarded with good spirits.
    Untill she basely yeelds, no ill inherits.

Moth. O happy child, 'faith, and thy birth hath saued me!
    'Mongst thousand daughters happiest of all others,
    Be thou a glasse for maides, and I for mothers.

                                                Exeunt.

ACT 5. SCNE. I.

Enter VINDICI *and* HIPPOLITO.

Vind. So, so! he leanes well. Take heede you wake him not, brother!

Hip. I warrant you my life for yours.

Vind. That's a good lay,—for I must kill my selfe! Brother, that's I: that fits for me; do you marke it. And I must stand ready here to make away my selfe yonder! I must sit to bee kild, and stand to kill my selfe! I could vary it not so little as thrice ouer agen; 'tas some eight returnes like Michelmas Tearme!

Hip. That's enow a' conscience!

Vind. But, sirrah, does the Duke's sonne come single?

Hip. No, there's the hell on't! his faith's too feeble to go alone! Hee brings flesh-flies after him, that will buzze against supper-time, and hum for his coming out.

Vind. Ah, the fly-flop of vengeance beate 'em to peeces! Here was the sweetest occasion, the fittest houre, to haue made my reuenge familiar with him!—show him the body of the Duke his father, and how quaintly he died like a Polititian in hugger-mugger, made no man acquainted with it ;—and in Catastrophe slay him ouer his father's brest—and oh, I'me mad to lose such a sweete opportunity!

Hip. Nay tush, pree-thee be content! there's no remedy present. May not hereafter times open in as faire faces as this?

Vind. They may, if they can paint so well.

Hip. Come now, to auoide all suspition, let's forsake this roome and be going to meete the Duke's sonne. *Ent.* Luss.

Vind. Content! I'me for any wether! 'Heart, step closse, here hee comes!

Hip. My honor'd Lord. *Luss.* O me! you both present?

Vind. E'en newly, my Lord—just as your Lordship enter'd now. About this place we had notice giuen hee should bee, but in some loathsome plight or other.

Hip. Came your honour priuate?

Luss. Priuate inough for this! onely a few
    Attend my comming out. *Hip.* Death rotte those
    few.   [Aside]

Luss. Stay, yonder's the slaue!

Vind. 'Masse, there's the slaue indeed, my Lord!
    'Tis a good child! he calls his Father slaue.

Luss. Aye, that's the villaine, the damnd villaine! Softly,
    Tread easie!

Vind. Pah, I warrant you, my Lord,
    Wee'll stifle in our breaths!

Luss. That will do well.
    Base rogue, thou sleepest thy last. 'Tis policie
    To haue him kild in's sleepe, for if he wakt
    Hee would betray all to them.

Vind. But, my Lord—— *Luss.* Ha, what sayst?

Vind. Shall we kill him now hee's drunke? *Luss.* Aye,
    best of all.

Vind. Why then hee will nere liue to be sober!

Luss. No matter; let him reele to hell.

Vind. But being so full of liquor I feare hee will put out
    all the fire.

Luss. Thou art a mad beast!

Vind. And leaue none to warme your Lordship's Golls withall. For he that dyes drunke falls into hell fire like a Bucket o'water, qush, qush!

Luss. Come, be ready; nake your swords; thinke of your wrongs!
This slaue has injur'd you.

Vind. Troth, so he has; and he has paide well for't.

Luss. Meete with him now.

Vind. You'll beare us out, my Lord?

Luss. Puh, am I a Lord for nothing, thinke you? Quickly now.

Vind. Sa, sa, sa! thumpe, there he lyes!

Luss. Nimbly done! ha!—Oh, villaines, murderers! 'Tis the old Duke my father! *Vind.* That's a jest.

Luss. What, stiffe and colde already?
O pardon me to call you from your names!
'Tis none of your deed.—That villaine Piato,
Whom you thought now to kill, has murder'd him,
And left him thus disguiz'd. *Hip.* And not unlikely.

Vind. O rascall! was he not asham'd
   To put the Duke into a greasie doublet?

Luss. He has beene cold and stiff, who knowes how
   long.

Vind. Marry, that do I! [Aside]

Luss. No words, I pray, of any thing intended.

Vind. Oh, my Lord!

Hip. I would faine haue your Lordship thinke that we
   haue small reason to prate.

Luss. 'Faith, thou say'st true! I'll forth-with send to
   Court
   For all the Nobles, Bastard, Duchesse, all;
   How here by miracle wee found him dead,
   And in his rayment that foule villaine fled.

Vind. That will be the best way, my Lord, to cleere us
   all: let's cast about to be cleere.

Luss. Ho, Nencio, Sordido, and the rest! *Enter all.*

1. *Servant.* My Lord. 2. *Servant.* My Lord.

Luss. Be witnesses of a strange spectacle!
   Choosing for priuate conference that sad roome,
   We found the Duke my father gealde in bloud.

1. *Servant.* My Lord the Duke!——Run, hie thee,
    Nencio;
    Startle the Court by signifying so much.

Vind. Thus much by wit a deep Reuenger can
    When murder's knowne; to be the cleerest man
    We're farthest off,—and with as bould an eye
    Suruay his body as the standers by.

Luss. My Royall father! too basëly let bloud
    By a maleuolent slaue!

Hip. Harke, he calls thee slaue agen! *Vind.* Has
    lost;—he may.

Luss. O sight, looke hether! his lips are gnawn with
    poyson!

Vind. How? his lips?—By th' masse they bee!

Luss. O villaine! O roague! O slaue! O rascall!

Hip. O good deceite, he quits him with like tearmes!

1. *Servant.* Where? 2. *Servant.* Which way?

Amb. Ouer what roofe hangs this prodigious Comet
    In deadly fire?

Luss. Behold, behold, my Lords, the Duke my father's
    murder'd by a vassail that owes this habit and
    here left disguisde!

Duch. My Lord and husband!   2. *Servant.* Reuerend
       Maiesty!

1. *Servant.* I haue seene these cloths often attending on
       him.

Vind. That Nobleman has bin i'th' Country, for he does
       not lie!

Sup. Learne of our mother: let's dissemble too.
       I am glad hee's vanisht; so I hope are you!

Amb. Aye, you may take my word for't.

Spur. Old Dad dead?
       I, one of his cast sinnes, will send the Fates
       Most hearty commendations by his owne sonne.
       I'll tug in the new streame till strength be done!

Luss. Where be those two that did affirme to us
       My Lord the Duke was priuately rid forth?

1. *Servant.* O pardon us, my Lords! hee gaue that charge,
       Upon our liues, if he were mist at Court
       To answer so: hee rode not any where;
       We left him priuate with that fellow here.

Vind. Confirmde!

Luss. O heauens, that false charge was his death!
       Impudent Beggars, durst you to our face

Maintaine such a false answer? Beare him straight
to execution.

1. *Servant.* My Lord! *Luss.* Urge me no more in this!
The excuse may be call'd halfe the murther.

Vind. Y'aue sentenc'd well!

Luss. Away, see it be done.

Vind. Could you not stick? See what confession doth!
Who would not lie when men are hang'd for truth?

Hip. Brother, how happy is our vengeance!

Vind. Why it hits,—
Past the apprehension of indifferent wits.

Luss. My Lord, let post horse be sent
Into all places to intrap the villaine.

Vind. Post-horse! ha, ha!

Nob. My Lord, we're some-thing bould to know our duty.
Your father's accidentally departed:
The titles that were due to him meete you.

Luss. Meete me? I'me not at leisure, my good Lord.
I'ue many greefes to dispatch out a'th' way.
Welcome sweete titles! Talke to me, my Lords,
Of sepulchers and mighty Emperor's bones.
That's thought for me.

Vind. So, one may see by this
    How forraine markets goe !
    Courtiers haue feete a'th' nines and tongues a'th'
        twellues ;
    They flatters Dukes and Dukes flatter them-selues.

Nob. My Lord, it is your shine must comfort us.

Luss. Alas, I shine in teares like the Sunne in Aprill.

Nob. You're now my Lord grace.

Luss. My Lord grace! I perceiue you'll haue it so.

Nob. 'Tis but your owne.

Luss. Then heauens giue me grace to be so !

Vind. He praies wel for him-selfe !

Nob. Madame, all sorrowes
    Must runne their circles into joyes. No doubt
        but time
    Wil make the murderer bring forth him-selfe.

Vind. He were an Asse then, y'faith !

Nob. In the meane season
    Let us bethinke the latest funerall-honors
    Due to the Duke's cold bodie,—and withall,
    Calling to memory our new happinesse,

Spreade in his royall sonne, Lords, Gentlemen,
Prepare for Reuells.   *Vind.* Reuells !

Nob. Time hath seuerall falls.
Greefes lift up joyes, feastes put downe funeralls.

Luss. Come then, my Lords, my fauors to you all.
The Duchesse is expected fowly bent.—
I'll beginne Dukedome with her banishment !

Hip. Reuells !   *Exeunt Duke, Nobles, and Duchesse.*

Vind. Aye, that's the word : we are firme yet !
Strike one straine more and then we crowne our wit.   *Exeu.* Bro.

Spu. Well, haue the fayrest marke—so said the Duke when he begot me,
And if I misse his heart or neere about,—
Then haue at any.   A Bastard scornes to be out !

Sup. Not'st thou that Spurio, brother ?

Amb. Yes, I note him to our shame.

Sup. He shall not liue, his haire shall not grow much longer ! In this time of Reuells tricks may be set a' foote. Seest thou yon new Moone ? It shall out-liue the Duke by much. This hand shall dispossesse him ; then we're mighty !

A maske is Treason's licence, that build upon ;
'Tis murder's best face when a vizard's on !
Exit SUPER.

Amb. Is't so ? 'Tis very good !
And do you thinke to be Duke then, kinde brother ?
I'll see faire play.———Drop one, and there lies t'other !   *Exit* AMBI.

[SCENE II.]

Enter VINDICI *and* HIPPOLITO, *with* PIERO *and other Lords.*

Vind. My Lords, be all of Musick : strike old griefs into other countries
That flow in too much milke, and haue faint liuers,
Not daring to stab home their discontents.
Let our hid flames breake out, as fire, as lightning,
To blast this villanous Dukedome vext with sinne.
Winde up your soules to their full height agen.

Piero. How ?   1. *Servant.* Which way ?

3. *Servant.* Any way. Our wrongs are such,
We cannot justly be reueng'd too much.

Vind. You shall haue all enough!—Reuels are toward,
    And those few Nobles that haue long suppress'd you
    Are busied to the furnishing of a Maske,
    And do affect to make a pleasant taile on't.
    The Masking suites are fashioning—now comes in
    That which must glad us all—wee to take patterne
    Of all those suites,—the colour, trimming, fashion,
    E'en to an undistinguisht hayre almost.
    Then ent'ring first, obseruing the true forme
    Within a straine or two, we shall finde leasure
    To steale our swords out handsomly;
    And when they thinke their pleasure sweete and good,
    In midst of all their joyes they shall sigh bloud!

Piero. Weightily! effectually!   3. *Servant.* Before the t'other Maskers come——

Vind. We're gone,—all done and past.

Piero. But how for the Duke's guard?   *Vind.* Let that alone.
    By one and one their strengths shall be drunke downe.

Hip. There are fiue hundred Gentlemen in the action,
    That will apply them-selues and not stand idle.

Piero. Oh, let us hug your bosomes! *Vind.* Come, my Lords,
    Prepare for deeds; let other times haue words.

Exeunt.

[SCENE III.]

In a dum shew the possessing of the young Duke with all his Nobles. Then sounding Musick. A furnisht table is brought forth; then enters the Duke and his Nobles to the banquet. A blasing-star appeareth.

Noble. Many harmonious houres and choisest pleasures
    Fill up the royall numbers of your yeares!

Luss. My Lords, we're pleas'd to thanke you; tho' we know
    'Tis but your duty now to wish it so.

Nob. That shine makes us all happy.

3. *Nob.* His Grace frounes!

2. *Nob.* Yet we must say he smiles. 1. *Nob.* I thinke we must.

Luss. That foule — incontinent Duchesse we haue banisht.

The Bastard shall not liue ! After these Reuells
I'll begin strange ones ! Hee and the stepsonnes
Shall pay their liues for the first subsidies.
We must not frowne so soone, else 't'ad beene now !

1. *Nob.* My gratious Lord, please you prepare for pleasure?
The maske is not far off.

Luss. We are for pleasure.
Beshrew thee, what art thou madst me start ?
Thou hast committed treason.—A blazing star !

1. *Nob.* A blazing star ! O where, my Lord ? *Luss.* Spy out.

2. *Nob.* See, see, my Lords, a wondrous-dreadfull one !

Luss. I am not pleas'd at that ill-knotted fire,
That bushing-staring star. Am I not Duke?
It should not quake me now ;—had it appear'd
Before, it I might then haue justly fear'd !
{ But yet they say, whom art and learning Weds,
{ When stars were locks they threaten great mens heads.
Is it so ? You are read, my Lords.

1. *Nob.* May it please your Grace,
   It showes great anger.

Luss. That does not please our Grace.

2. *Nob.* Yet here's the comfort, my Lord.   Many times
   When it seemes most, it threatens farthest off.

Luss. Faith, and I thinke so too!

1. *Nob.* Beside, my Lord,
   You're gracefully establisht with the loues
   Of all your subjects ; and for naturall death,
   I hope it will be threescore years a comming.

Luss. True, no more but threescore years!

1. *Nob.* Fourescore I hope, my Lord.   2. *Nob.* And fiue-
   score I.

3. *Nob.* But 'tis my hope, my Lord, you shall nere die.

Luss. Giue me thy hand ; these others I rebuke.
   He that hopes so is fittest for a Duke!
   Thou shalt sit next me. Take your places, Lords:
   We're ready now for sports ; let 'em set on.
   You thing, we shall forget you quite anon!

3. *Nob.* I heare 'em comming, my Lord.

Enter the Maske of Reuengers: the two Brothers and two Lords more.

Luss. Ah, 'tis well!
    Brothers and Bastard, you dance next in hell!

The Reuengers daunce.
At the end steale out their swords, and these foure kill the foure at Table in their Chaires. It thunders.

Vind. Marke, Thunder!
    Dost know thy kue, thou big-voyc'st cryer?
    Dukes groanes are thunder's watch-words.

Hip. So, my Lords! You haue ynough!

Vind. Come, let's away! No lingring!   *Exeunt.*

Hip. Follow, goe!

Vind. No power is angry when the lust-ful die.
    When thunder claps heauen likes the tragedy.
                         Exit VIND.

Luss. Oh, oh!

Enter the other Maske of extended murderers—Stepsons, Bastard, and a fourth man—comming in dauncing. The Duke recouers a little in voyce and groanes—calls a guard, treason.

At which they all start out of their measure, and turning towards the Table they finde them all to be murdered.

Spur. Whose groane was that? *Luss.* Treason, a guard!

Amb. How now, all murder'd? *Super.* Murder'd!

4. *Noble.* And those his Nobles!

Amb. Here's a labour sau'd!
I thought to haue sped him. 'Sbloud, how came this?

Spur. Then I proclaime my selfe, now I am Duke.

Amb. Thou Duke! brother, thou liest!

Spur. Slaue, so dost thou!

4. *Noble.* Base villayne, has thou slaine my Lord and Maister?

Enter the first men.

Vind. Pistolls, treason, murder! Help, guard my Lord the Duke!

Hip. Lay hold upon this Traytor! *Luss.* Oh!

Vind. Alasse, the Duke is murder'd! *Hip.* And the Nobles!

Vind. Surgeons, Surgeons!—Heart, do'es he breath so long!

Ant. A piteous tragædy, able to make
An old man's eyes bloud-shot! *Luss.* Oh!

Vind. Looke to my Lord the Duke! (A vengeance throttle him!)
Confesse, thou murdrous and unhallowed man,
Didst thou kill all these?

4. *Noble.* None but the Bastard I.

Vind. How came the Duke slaine then?

4. *Noble.* We found him so. *Luss.* O villaine!

Vind. Harke! *Luss.* Those in the maske did murder us

Vind. La' you now sir.
O marble impudence, will you confesse now?

4. *Noble.* 'Slud, 'tis all false!

Ant. Away with that foule monster
Dipt in a Prince's bloud.

4. *Noble.* 'Heart, 'tis a lye!

Ant. Let him haue bitter execution.

Vind. New marrow, no I cannot be exprest. [Aside
How faires my Lord the Duke?

Luss. Farewel to all.

He that climes highest has the greatest fall.—
My tong is out of office.

Vind. Ayre, Gentlemen, ayre!
Now thou'lt not prate on't!——'twas *Vindici*
murdred thee.

Luss. Oh!   *Vind.* Murdred thy Father.

Luss. Oh! [Dies]

Vind. And I am "he-tell no-body." So, so! the Duke's
departed!

Ant. It was a deadly hand that wounded him!
The rest, ambitious who should rule and sway
After his death, were so made all away.

Vind. My Lord was unlikely. *Hip.* Now the hope
Of Italy lyes in your reuerend yeares.

Vind. Your hayre will make the siluer age agen,
When there were fewer, but more honest men.

Ant. The burden's weighty and will presse age downe.
May I so rule that heauen may keepe the crowne

Vind. The rape of your good Lady has beene quited
With death on death. *Ant.* Just is the Lawe
aboue!

But of all things it puts me most to wonder
How the old Duke came murder'd. *Vind.* O my Lord!

Ant. It was the strangeliest carried! I'ue not heard of the like.

Hip. 'Twas all donne for the best, my Lord.

Vind. All for your Grace's good! We may be bould to speake it now.
'Twas some-what witty carried, tho' we say it.
'Twas we two murder'd him. *Ant.* You two?

Vind. None else i'faith, my Lord. Nay, 'twas well manag'd!

Ant. Lay hands upon those villaines! *Vind.* How? On us?

Ant. Beare 'em to speedy execution.

Vind. 'Heart, was't not for your good, my Lord?

Ant. My good! Away with'em! Such an ould man as he!
You that would murder him would murder me.

Vind. Is't come about? *Hip.* 'Sfoote, brother, you begun!

Vind. May not we set as well as the Duke's sonne?
 Thou hast no conscience; are we not reueng'd?
 Is there one enemy left aliue amongst those?
 'Tis time to die when we're our selues our foes.
 When murders shut deeds closse, this curse does
    seale 'em,
 If none disclose 'em they themselues reueale 'em!
 This murder might haue slept in tonglesse brasse,
 But for our selues, and the world dyed an asse.
 Now I remember too here was Piato
 Brought a knauish sentance once—no doubt (said
    he) but time
 Will make the murderer bring forth himselfe!
 'Tis well he died : he was a witch.
 And now, my Lord, since we are in for euer
 This worke was ours, which else might haue beene
    slipt.
 And if we list we could haue Nobles clipt,
 And goe for lesse than beggers; but we hate
 To bleed so cowardly. We haue ynough!
 Y'faith, we're well—our Mother turn'd—our Sister
    true;
 We die after a nest of Dukes,—adieu!   *Exeunt.*

Ant. How subtilly was that murder clos'd! Beare up
Those tragick bodies. 'Tis a heauy season!
Pray heauen their bloud may wash away all
treason! *Exit.*

FINIS.

NOTES TO THE REUENGER'S TRAGÆDIE.

ACT I.

This first scene Tourneur modelled no doubt on Chettle's *Hoffman's Tragedy*, where the hero Hoffman is represented as soliloquising over the skeleton of his murdered father and swearing to revenge him. Venici stands of course with the skull of his murdered mistress in his hand, and is doubtless on the upper stage, which was a balcony raised eight or ten feet from the ground (see among many others Middleton's *Family of Love*, act i. sc. iii., and Dyce's note; also *Witch*, act iv. sc. iii.), while the other characters pass along the ordinary stage below him.

Should stuffe. A necessary emendation for the *would* c quartos.

A parch'd and juiceless luxur.

Luxury was the term used to express incontinence, the Lat *uria*. Cf. Shakespeare, *passim*, and Middleton's *Game of C* "In a room fill'd all with Aretine's pictures more than the tw. labours of *Luxury*;" and Fletcher's *Purple Island*, vii. 20 :

"With sweltering heart in flames of *Luxury*."

Luxur means therefore a person given to lust or luxury.

And what his father fifty yearès told.

This lengthened syllable is a trace of the old English still lingering on; among many other instances see Shakespeare's *Rich. II.*, iii. iii. 9 :

> " Your Grace mistakès, only to be brief
> Left I his title out ;"

and First Part of *Henry VI.* i. iii. 5 :

> " Who's there that knockès so imperiously?"

See too Abbott's *Shakespearian Grammar*, p. 385.

Tourneur is fond of it. Cf. *infra:*

> " The Dutches sonnés are too proud to bleed."
> "Not since two hourés before noon, my Lord."
> " To this our lecherous hope the Dukés son."
> " Nimble and desperate tongués should we name."

Told, *i.e.* counted.

Costly three-pil'd flesh.

Three-pile was the most delicate and costly kind of velvet. The Dramatists are full of allusions to it. Cf. *Winter's Tale*, iv. ii. ; *My World, my Masters*, act i. :

> " I'll tell him how you wish it, and I'll wear
> My wits to the *third pile*."

'or the adjective in metaphorical sense, cf. Fletcher's *Scornful ly*, iii. i. :

> You snuff at all but *three-pil'd* people ;"

Measure for Measure, i. ii. ; *Love's Labour's Lost*, v. ii.

Has that bald Madame, etc.

Mr. Hazlitt will I hope forgive me relieving the dulness of these notes by recording his reading of this line, " Has that *bald madman* opportunity, etc." Had it not been for what follows some lines afterwards one might be tempted to conjecture *bawd*. Cf. Heywood's *Faire Maide of the West*, act i.

> "Win *oportunity*
> She's the *best bawd*."

Or like the French mole, etc.

This is of course an allusion to one of the usual effects of the *Lues Venerea*. It would be impertinent to cite any of the innumerable references to this and other effects of the disease to be found in the old dramatists, though it may not be impertinent to refer to Fracastorius' magnificent poem entitled *Syphilis*, or Francesca Maria Molza's exquisite elegies. But see Gifford's note on "You should give him a French crown for it," in Ben Jonson's *Every Man out of his Humour*.

Wives are but made, etc.

So thought Euripides, who preferred, however, like Palladas, the alternative of burying to feeding them :

> "Πᾶσα γυνή χόλος ἐστ' ἀγαθάς 'ἔχεται δύο ὥρας
> Τήν μίαν ἐν θαλάμῳ, τήν μίαν ἐν θανάτῳ,"

Yu'll bring me onward, *i.e.*, accompany or escort. Cf. Heywood's *Woman Killed with Kindness:*

"And she went very lovingly *to bring him on his way* to horse."

Insculption, *i.e.* to carve or engrave. Cf. Massinger's *Bashful Lover*, act iv. sc. i. :

> "A glorious name
> *Insculped* on pyramids to eternity ;"

and *Merchant of Venice*, act ii. sc. vii.

Boweld corps, *i.e.*, disembowelled. It was usual to take out the intestines for the sake of embalming the corpse.

Should take fast hold. Quartos read *first.* I alter with Reed and Collier.

Why flesh and blood, my Lord.

Provokes an allusion to Fra Lippi Lippo, who makes use of the same words in circumstances which may possibly have led to the same climax.

She's a godess, for I'd no power to see her and to live.

A gracefully profane allusion to the preposterous epiphany in Exodus xxxiii.

I might be easier *sess'd.* The quartos read *ceas'd.*

Your too much right, etc.

A reminiscence of Cicero, *De Officiis* i. 10: "Summum jus, summa injuria factum est jam tritum sermone proverbium." Cf. also *Jew of Malta*, act i. :

"Your extreme *right* does me exceeding wrong."

For the same play on the words cf. Sophocles, *Œd. Rex*, 1067-8

" Τὰ λῷστα σοι λέγω
 Τὰ λῷστα τοινυν ταῦτα μ'ἀλγύνει πάλαι."

That jewel's mine, etc.

It was common at that time for men to wear earrings. Cf. *Every Man in His Humour*, act iv. sc. vii. :

" *Mathew.* I'll pawn this jewel in my ear."

Cf. also *Malcontent*, i. 6, and *King and No King*, act i. sc. i.

As to a hatted dame.

A woman of the lower orders, who wore hats at this time, as the Welsh women do now. See Hollar's picture in his *Ornatus Muliebris.*

He had his length, i'faith, etc.

This is a difficult passage, owing to the uncertainty of the punctuation, for the punctuation of the quartos is, in almost all cases where there is ambiguity, worthless. I explain thus. The passage begin with an obscene double entendre, and then proceeds, "He was wondrous tall, he had his length, i'faith." For, or because, he peeped over half-shut holiday-windows when on horseback, men would desire him to alight from his horse : or placing a comma after "for," it may be taken, "Men who were peeping over half-shut holiday windows, seeing him where he ought not to be, would desire him to alight," referring to the former double entendre. See the next note. But the passage may obviously be taken in many ways, according to the punctuation. It would delight a German commentator. A penthouse was a kind of hat common at the time.

Nay, set you a horseback once.

An obvious allusion to the proverb, "Set a beggar on horseback and he'll ride a gallop."

To the illustrations added by Dodsley's first editor :

" Asperius nihil est humili quum surgit in altum, Claudian ;

" Il n'est orgueil qui de pauvre enrichi ;"

" Il villan nobililado non conosce il parentado ;"

add Æschylus, *Prometh. Vinct.* 35,

"Ἄπας δὲ τραχὺς οστις ἀν νέον κρατῇ,"

and *Measure for Measure,* act i. sc. iii., "Or whether that the body," etc. Though I am afraid the double entendre of the Latin *equitare* of the Aristophanic κελητίζειν, of the German *reiten,* and of the French *chevaucher* is more to the point in this passage.

In thy thought, etc. "Thy" is omitted by the quartos, supplied by the editors.

Drops out of the collet.

The setting which surrounds the stone of a ring. See Nares' excellent note in his Glossary.

Seventh commandement.

For the lengthening of the syllable, cf. with Abbott :

" If to women he be hent,
   They have at commandément ;"

and Ben Jonson, *Fox*, iii. 2 :

"Good sir, you'll give them entertainément ;"

and the note on "yearés," etc.

I'll harm thy brow with woman's heraldry.

I.e., The ornament of which Benedict, *Much Ado About Nothing*, act i. sc. i., had such a horror, and for an illustration see a few lines further.

I'll loose my dayes upon him.

There is something wrong here. Either we must boldly conjecture "rage" for days, or read lose for loose, *i.e.*, I'll waste my time on him, devote my life to revenging myself on him, by idling away my time in committing adultery, etc. I do not alter the text because it may be a bold figure, for meaning I will loose the whole action of my life like a hound from the leash upon him.

Would never suffer her to get good clothes.

A sarcastic commentary on a common classical epithet, *nuda*, applied respectively to Simplicitas, Veritas, and Fides.

Save Grace the bawd.

The same pun runs through Heywood's *Wise Woman of Hogsdon*, and is applied there to a character alternately styled Grace and Gratiana.

Words are but great men's blanks.

Blanks are bonds. Cf. Ben Jonson, *Every Man Out of His Humour*, act iv. sc. iv. : "The children of darkness all day in a melancholy shop with their pockets full of *blanks*."

As would gravel a petition.

An allusion to throwing sand on wet ink to dry it, the common expedient before the invention of blotting-paper.

Next to the rim o' th' sister.

"That is, no degree of relationship is sufficient to restrain the appetite of lust, scarce that of sister; they even approach to the rim or verge of what is most prohibited."—Dodsley, original note. I am ashamed, though forced, to suspect that there is an allusion to *Juv. Sat.* iii. 97. See too Nares' art. *Rim.*

In sooth it is too.

The editors read "true ;" but there is no reason for altering if we take it as an aposiopesis. He was going to say "It is too true," but he suddenly interrupts himself.

Though hell gap't wide.

Quartos read "loud," a printer's error, easily accounted for.

This Indian devil.

Money. India being synonymous with the land of riches. Cf. *Transform'd Metamorphosis*, passim.

What breeds a loathing, etc.

See Savage's *Bastard*, lines 30—40, for a pertinent comment.

A stock of money laid to sleep.

Cf. the Italian commercial phrase, *lasciar star morti*, as applied to money; and see an excellent note on the Italian commercial phrases which have passed into literary parlance in Rose's *Ariosto*, vol. iv. p. 46.

To wind up a good fellow.

A thief who is going to steal his sister's chastity. Good fellow was the ordinary phrase for a thief. Cf. *A Trick to Catch the Old One*, act ii. sc. i. :

"*Luc.* Welcome, *good fellow.*
Host. He calls me thief at first sight ;"

and Heywood, *Edward IV.*, part i. :

" Dost thou not love *good fellows ?*
No, 'tis a bye-word : *good fellows* are *thieves.*"

The name is so in league with age, etc.

I can only explain this by supposing that *th'* must have dropped out. Read,

"The name is so in league with th' age, that now adaies
   It does eclipse," etc.

The name (of bawd) is so closely connected with every woman in the age in which we live that even a mother is naturally three parts of one already.

Upon their blood. The quartos read "good," a slip probably of the printer's. Blood = of course, disposition.

"Melius virtute mori, quam per dedecus vivere."

This is from the Fragments of the *Pirithous* of Euripides :

"οὐκοῦν τὸ μὴ ζῆν κρεῖττόν ἐστ᾽ ἢ ζῆν κακῶς,"

though Tourneur probably got it from some more familiar source.

"*Curæ leves loquuntur, ingentes stupent,*"

a. is a trite quotation from Seneca, or whoever wrote the plays attributed to him.

When torchlight made an artificial noon,

Looks like a reminiscence of Æschylus, *Agamemnon,* 22 :

"λαμπτὴρ νυκτὸς ἡμερήσιον φάος πιφαύσκων."

He harry'd her.

From Norman French *harier*, to vex, torment, or pull rudely Cf. *Ant. and Cleop.*, act ii. sc. iii. :

"Indeed he is so, I repent me much
That I so *harried* him."

It probably means here plunder or ravish. Cf. the Scotch phrase and cf. too Ford, *Lady's Trial*, act ii. sc. ii. :

"Would all their spite could *harry* my contents
Into a desperate ruin."

ACT II.

Lady, the best of wishes, etc.

Of this whole scene down to "Why that was motherly said,

Lamb says, " The reality and life of this dialogue passes any scenical allusion I ever felt. I never read it but my ears tingle, and I feel a hot blush spread my cheeks as if I were presently about to 'proclaim' some such malefactions of myself as the brothers here relate in their unnatural parent, in words more keen and dagger-like than those which Hamlet speaks to his mother. Such power has the passion of shame truly personated not only to strike guilty creatures unto the soul, but to 'appal' even those who are 'free.'"

Our mighty expectation. A literal translation of Virgil's *Magnæ spes altera Romæ.*

The crown gapes for him every tide.

Tide is the old word for time; cf. *Timon of Athens*, i. 2, "He keeps his tides well," and all that is meant here, is the crown is every day expecting to pass into his hands. Cf. Lat. *inhiare*, and the common use of it.

Men have no power, angels must work you to't.

An angel was a gold coin worth about 10*s*. This play on the word is one of the stock jokes of the old dramatists.

While others clip the sun.

Embrace. Cf. *Winter's Tale*, v. 2., " Then again worries he thy daughter with *clipping* her ;" and *infra*, " Here in this lodge they meet for damned *clips*."

Petitionary people. Cf. Marston, *Malcontent*, act i. sc. v., " Petitionary vassals licking the pavement with their slavish knees."

An you were there. The quartos read "and." I have ventured to expunge a letter, as *and* and *an* are frequently confused.

But let horns wear 'em.

I.e., who had not the privilege of entering presence chambers with their hats on, but were obliged to hang them in the hall on the stags' horns hung there. There is of course a double entendre latent.

Walk with a hundred acres on their back.
For this conceit cf. *Miseries of Inforc'd Marriage*, "I that hav[e] made them that have worn a spacious park, lodge, and all on thei[r] backs this morning," etc.; and Lodge's *Wit's Misery*, "What thin[k] you to a tender, fair, young, nay, a weakling of womankind, to wea[r] whole lordships and manor houses on her back without sweating?" and cf. *Henry VIII.*, act i. sc. i., and for a humorous point mad[e] out of it, Addison, *Spectator*, No. 295.

Mete by the rod.
Measured by the measuring-rod. The point is obvious.

She's too inward then. Too much identified with yourself.

Which I never learned in schools. Yet he might have learned i[t] from a Greek cynic's definition of a πόλις.

Knave in your face, my lord, behind your back.
This can only be explained as a somewhat obscure aposiopesis.

I bate in courage now.
Decline, lessen. Cf. *Henry IV.*, part i. act iii. 2, "Do I not *bate*, do I not dwindle."

White money, i.e., silver.

Beg, leg. Bow, crouch, duck low. There is no reason for altering the text.

And all the farthingales, etc.
Cf. Ben Jonson, *Cynthia's Revels*, act iii. sc. i., "All the ladies and gallants lie languishing upon the rushes like so many pounded cattle."

Apprehensive. Quick to understand. Cf. Falstaffe on sherris-sack. "It makes it [the brain] *apprehensive*, quick," etc. Cf. too Ben Jonson, *Every Man out of His Humour:*

"You are too quick, too *apprehensive*."

Thou that lookst like funeral heralds' fees.
Fees is doubtless put for phease or pheese, which means tatters or hangings, being a substantive derived from the verb. In this

place then it would mean the black frieze put up on the occasion of a funeral, which remaining for the night was taken down next morning. See Wedgewood, article *fease*.

Are now perhaps i' the toll-book.

"This is an allusion to the common custom of entering horses sold at a fair in a book called the toll-book."—Dodsley. See Steeven's note on "I will buy me a son-in-law in a fair and toll for this."—*All's Well that Ends Well*, act v. sc. iii.

Among the lawyars,—Guard. The quartos' "Lawyer's guard," will make no sense.

File my lips with.

For defile. Cf. *Macbeth*, act i. 3, i., "For Banquo's issue have I 'fil'd my mind," with the references there given.

Vildlier done. Vild, a common form of vile.

And I am woe for you.

I am sorry for you. Cf. *Tempest*, 5, i. :

"I am woe for't, sir ;"

and Heywood's *Four P's* :

"But be ye sure *I would be woe*
If ye shulde chance to beguile me so."

Peevish moon.

"Some sudden fit of frenzy. Cotgrave translates 'Avoir un quartier de la lune en la teste,' to be half frantic, or have a spice of lunacy.—Dodsley. Rather the same as *lunes*, moods; cf. *Merry Wives of Windsor*, act iv. sc. ii., "Why woman your husband is in his old *lunes* again ;" and cf. *As You Like It*, act iii. sc. ii. :

"I buy but a *moonish* youth."

Here's envy.

Lat. *invidia*, enmity, hatred. Cf. *Merchant of Venice*, iv. i. :

"No lawful means can carry me
Out of his *envy's* reach."

Cf. too, Reynold's *Revenge against Murder*:

"He never looks on her with affection, but *envy*."

ACT III.

Blest occasion. Quartos read "blast."

Put. A necessary correction for the "but" of the quartos.

And set an edge upon, etc. Cf. Horace, *Ars Poetic.* 402, "Mares animos in martia bella *exacuit*."

Bigger block.

Block is properly the wooden mould on which the crown of a hat was formed. Sometimes used, as here, for the hat itself. Cf. Beaumont and Fletcher, *Martial Maid*, "Though now your blockhead be covered with a Spanish *block*. Cf. also *Lear*, iv. vi.

A villainous Duns.

An allusion to Duns Scotus, the subtlest of the schoolmen who commented upon the *Magister Sententiarum*. He is here of course identified with a subtle interpreter. Cf. *New Custom*, 1573:

"I could smatter *in a Duns* prettelie for fortie yeares ago."

You know a trick is commonly four cards.

This is an allusion to the popular game of primero. Nothing can be added to Nares' excellent and lucid account of this game in his *Glossary*, which I could but reproduce.

And knock his forehead, etc. Horace's "sublimi feriam vertic sidera." Od. I. i.

Shadowing vices.' Cf. "Thy bastard ev'n now *shadows* the Duchess," act ii. last scene.

White device. Hoary. For another curious use of this word se Dyce's note on "my *white* hat," Webster's *Northward Ho*, act iv sc. i.

Not like a flobbering Dutchman.

And yet it was a Dutchman who had reduced the pastime to a science, though Tourneur may be excused for having forgotten or ignored Johannes Secundus.

I—'tis Vindici. Aristotle has somewhere remarked that revenge is not complete, unless the agent declares himself. Those who are familiar with the ethics of barbarous nations will be at no loss for parallel illustrations.

To stick thy soul with ulcers.

This striking and terrific image is to be found in, and may have been borrowed from, Plato, *Gorgias*, cap. lxxx., where he speaks of a "ψυχὴ διαμεμαστυγωμένη κὰι ουλῶν μεστὴ ὑπὸ ἐπιορκιῶν κὰι ἀδικίας."

Haspt—i.e., in the very act, in ipsâ pyxide.

ACT IV.

Rac'd my father's bosom. I alter ras'd, *i.e.*, grazed or scratch'd. Cf. "Ras'd their harden'd hides."—*Harrison;* see Halliwell's *Glossary*.

And all about pullen and pigs.

Pullen. Poultry. Cf. Beaumont and Fletcher, *Scornful Lady*, v. ii., "She candies pretty well in the pastry and knows how *pullen* should be crammed."

Where we greet in fire, etc.

Graphic, and to be understood not by analysis but impression. It is in fact one of those constructions *ad sensum* so common in Sophocles, and sometimes affected by Tennyson. Cf.:

"There with her milk-white arms and shadowy hair
She made her face a darkness from the king."
Guinevere.

Where the general sense is cleare, but where analysis makes nonsense.

Sasarara. This is a corruption of *certiorari*, the title of a legal writ by which a proceeding is removed to a higher court; it is spe[lt] "siserara" and "seserara." Cf. *The Puritan*, iii. 3; and Middl[e]ton, *The Phœnix*, act i. sc. iv. : " O rapturous, here's a writ of demu[r] and there a procedendo, here a *sursurrara*."

Had rather be damn'd indeed than damn'd in colours.
Would rather be damn'd outright than be damned in the eyes [of] their fellow-creatures by being made ridiculous in a bad picture.

Money t' has been my want so long, etc.
Cf. Congreve, *Love for Love*, act i. sc. i., "I have no money, y[et] know it, and therefore resolve to laugh at all who have."

To me seems proud, i.e., excessive, as often.

To quit. Requite, as often.

But with some fine. The quartos read five, which not understan[d]ing, I reluctantly alter to what is a flat but obvious correction.

Is there no thunder left, etc.
Cf. *Othello*, v. 2 :

"Are there no stones in heaven
But what serve for the thunder?"

and Sophocles, *Electra* 825;

"Ποῦ ποτε κεραυνοὶ Διός ἤ
Που φαέθων Ἅλιος, ἐι
Ταῦτ' ἐφορῶντες
Κρύπτουσιν ἕκηλοι."

Sluggy. Old form for sluggish.

Shall when he's known, etc. This passage appears to be ho[pe]lessly corrupt. I adopt Mr. Collier's reading We for me.

Most women have small waste, etc. A Shakespearian pun. [Cf.] Sec. Part *Henry IV.* i. ii.

O thou for whom, etc. See Charles Lamb's eloquent criticism [of] this scene.

Oh are sons turned masters, etc.
This closely resembles a passage in Æschylus, *Chœphorœ*, 883 *seq.*:

"ἐπίσχες ὦ παῖ τόν δε αἴδεσαι, τέκνον,
μαστὸν, πρὸς ᾧ σὺ πολλὰ δὴ βρίζων ἅμα
οὔλοισιν ἐξήμελξας ἐντραφὲς γάλα."

The position in the two plays is very similar.

Quarled poison.
I am sorry I can suggest nothing better than Nares' interpretation: that it may mean subtle poison such as was put on quarles or quarrels (*i.e.*, square darts) to make them more deadly; and so meaning the most rancorous poison. Mr. Halliwell Phillips in his *Glossary* needlessly proposes gnarled poison, which scarcely mends matters. The Italian practice of poisoning saddles, whip-handles, daggers, etc., so often alluded to by our dramatists, bears out the probability that Nares' interpretation is right, as it is certainly sensible.

Ah is it possible. The punctuation of the quartos makes simply nonsense; there is an ellipse, Is it possible that you only hate it?

To give aim to her own daughter.
This phrase, meaning to incite, encourage, or assent to, is properly a metaphorical application of the term *to cry aim*, which was employed in archery to encourage the archers. See Warburton's note on "Cry aim, said I well."—*Merry Wives of Windsor*, ii. iii. Cf. for the literal sense Webster's *Villoria Corombona*:

"I'll *give aim* to you
And tell you how to shoot;"

and in Cooke's Green's *Tu Quoque*:

"We'll stand by, and *give aim*, and haloo if you hit the clout."

For the metaphorical sense see Middleton's *Faire Quarrel*, i. i.:

"How now, gallants?
Believe me then, I must *give aim* no longer."

We will make iron blush. The quarto of 1607 reads "You blush;' I adopt the reading of the last quarto, 1608 : it must be remembered that Vindici is addressing his sword as he sheathes it.

Seld and rare. Seldom to be met with. Cf. Kyd's *Cornelia* act i.

" So that we *seld* are seen as wisdom would ;"

and Shakespeare, *Coriolanus*, ii. i. :

" *Seld shown* flamens do press among the popular throngs."

To have her train borne up and her soul trail i' the dirt.
Mr. Gerald Massey has appropriated or hit upon this striking and beautiful image in his *Babe Christabel:*

" Then lest her starry garments trail
   In mire," etc.

I think man's happiest, etc.
There are few men of genius who have not left commentaries, in some form or other, on this melancholy line.

Be thou a glass, etc. " A mirrour for maids and mothers to dress themselves by." Cf. Shakespeare, "*glass* of fashion." Quarto reads *Buy.* I alter.

ACT V.

Some eight returns like Michaelmas term.
This term had eight returns, but a statute of 16 Car. I., and another 24 George II., reduced it to four.

Ah the fly-flop of vengeance. Cf. *Lear*, act iv. sc. i.:

" As flies to wanton boys are we to the gods ;
   They kill us for their sport."

He died like a polititian in hugger mugger.
In secret ; an old word of very doubtful etymology. Cf. *Hamlet*

> "And we have done but greenly
> In hugger-mugger to inter him ;"

and cf. North's *Plutarch:* " Antonius thinking that his body should be honourably buried, and not in *hugger-mugger ;*" and in the *Satiromastrix:* "One word, Sir Quintilian, in *hugger mugger.*"

I strongly suspect that this is a misprint for Politian, the celebrated Italian scholar, who is so identified with Lorenzo de Medici. The various stories which were reported about his somewhat mysterious death would probably impress Tourneur. His name moreover was familiar to playgoers. See Lyly's *Sappho and Phaon*, act i. sc. iv. : " Wee pages are Politians, for looke what wee heare," etc. ; and cf. Halliwell, note in loc.

Golls. Hands or paws, usually a contemptuous expression. Cf. Middleton's *Chaste Maide in Cheapside:*

> " What their *golls*
> Can clutch goes presently to their Molls and Dolls."

Cf. *Honest Whore,* i. iv. :

> " Done, 'tis a lay, join *golls* on't ;"

and Massinger, *City Madam,* iv. i. :

> " Ambitious to shake the golden *golls*
> Of worshipful Mrs. Luke."

Nake your swords. The quarto of 1607 reads *make.* Make your swords naked ; unsheathe. The obsolete verb of which naked is the past participle. Cf. *Aminta,* quoted by Nares :

> " Thrice the green field
> Hath the *nak'd* scythman barbed."

Too basëly let blood. For the lengthening of the syllable, cf. Shakespeare, *Tempest,* iii. iii. 40 :

> " *Fran.* They vanish'd strangëly.
> *Seb.* No matter."

For similar licences see Shakespeare, *Sonnet* lxvi., "and strength by limping is disabled, and *Two Gentlemen of Verona*, I. iii., "C how the spring of love resembleth," cf. also Malone's note in the passage.

Prodigious comet. Portentous. Cf. *Honest Whore*, i. i. :

"Yon comet shews his head again.
Twice hath he thus at cross-turns thrown on us
Prodigious looks;"

and *King John*, iii. i., and the references of the commentators.

Talk to me, etc. Compare Shakespeare, *Rich. II.*, act iii. sc. ii. :

"Let's *talk* of graves," etc.

Time hath several falls. Time puts on many veils or guises. See note on *Atheist's Tragedy*, act iv. sc. i. It may be explained, no doubt, by "Time falls out variously," or again as a metaphor from the dice, in which case cf. Æschylus, *Agamemnon* :

"Ταῦτα δ'ἐν πολλῷ χρονῳ
Τὰ μέν τις εὖ λέξειεν εὐπετῶς ἔχειν
Τὰ δ'αὖτε κἀπίμομφα."

You that would murder him, etc.

There is a curious resemblance between this and Sophocles, *Œd. Rex*, 135 :

"Ἀλλ' αὐτὸς αὑτοῦ τοῦτ' ἀποσκεδῶ μύσος
Ὅστις γὰρ ἦν ἐκεῖνον ὁ κτανὼν τάχ' ἂν
Κἄμ ἂν τοιαύτῃ χειρὶ τιμωρεῖν θέλοι."

Tongueless. Another echo from *Rich. II.*, i. i.

"Even from the *tongueless* caverns of the earth.

THE
TRANSFORMED
METAMORPHOSIS

By *CYRIL TURNER*

Malo virum pecunia quam pecuniam viro indigentem

Printed by *VALENTINE SIMS*, and are to be
Sold at the Signe of the White Swan
on Adling hill
1600

Pursue the bloudy that doth robbe the poore.
And drowns the orphants in their purple goare.

So shall thy race, wherein thou hast begunne
In heaven end, for which thou so dost runne.

To the right Worshipfull
SIR CHRISTOPHER HEYDON, C. T.
WISHETH ÆTERNALL FRUITION
OF ALL FELICITIE.

Thou, thou that art the Muses' Adonie
Their Pyramis, adorner of their mount,
Thou Christalizer of their Castalie,
Thou Lillian-rose, sprung from the horse-foote fount.
To thee, Arte's Patron, Champion to the highest
That givest the sunne a fairer radiance;
To thee, Musophilus, that still appliest
Thy sacred soule, to be Truthe's esperance,
To thee this Epinyctall register
Rasde out by Eos rayes I write to thee.
To thee this hoarie Hiems kill'd by Ver,
To thee this metamorphosed Tragædie,
To thee I write my Apotheosie
Mæcenas, strengthen my Tyrocinie.

                Your Worships ever
                    CYRILL TURNER.

THE AUTHOR TO HIS BOOKE

O were Thy margents cliffes of itching lust
Or quotes to chalke out men the way to sin;
Then were there hope that multitudes wold thrust
To buy thee: but sith that thou dost beginne
To pull the curtaines backe that closde vice in
Expect but flowts, for t'is the haire of crime
To shunne the breath that doth discloude it sinne.
What? will he say a recluse from the time?
Nor canst thou hope that thy weake joynted rime
Shall please the more, because it shrowdes itselfe
Under his shade whose mighty armes do clime
Ev'n to the highest heav'n, disdaining pelfe;
For heavenly mindes, the brightlier they do shine
The more the world doth seeke to work their tine:
This only be thy hope,—to please the best
And to be safe from malice of the rest.

TO THE READER.

It may be (Reader) I may gall those men
Whose golden thoughts thinke no man dare them touch;
It may be too my fearelesse ayre-plume-pen
May rouse that sluggish watch whose tongues are such
As are controll'd by feare or gold too much:
Yet were Apelles here, he could not paint
Forth perfectly the world's deformities.
For as the troubled mind whose sad complaint
Still tumbles forth half-breathed accenties,
Th' *Idea* doth confuse and chaoize:
So will the *Chaos* of up-heaped sinne
Confound his braine that takes in hand to lay
A platforme plainly forth, of all that in
This Pluto-visag'd world hell doth bewray,
When death or hell doth worke it lives decay.
So perfect is our imperfectionesse
For imperfection is sinne's perfectnesse.

Yet seeke I not to touch as he that seekes
The publike defamation of some one;
Nor have I spent my voide houres in three weekes
To shew that I am unto hatred prone;
For in particular I point at none:
Nay I am forced my lines to limit in
Within the pale of generalitie:
For should I seeke by unites to begin
To point at all that in their sinne do lie
And hunt for wickedness advisedly,
As well I then might go about to tell
The perfect number of the Ocean sands,
Or by Arithmetike goe downe to hell
And number them that lie in horror's bands,
(Ne're to be ransom'd from the diuell's hands).
Who finds him touch't may blame himself not me
And he will thanke me, doth himselfe know free.

                Thine as I see thy affection
                      CYRILL TURNER.

INTRODUCTION.

SIR CHRISTOPHER HEYDON, to whom this poem is dedicated, was the son of Sir W. Heydon, and belonged to a very old family, familiar to the readers of the Paston Letters. He was educated at Cambridge, and on leaving the University travelled on the Continent, and probably also in Italy. He served under Essex, and was knighted by him at the sacking of Cadiz in 1596. On his return to England he was high steward of the Cathedral Church of Norwich. It appears that both he and his brother were engaged in Essex's rebellion, and a pardon was issued for them, as well as many others, in 1601. He subsequently devoted himself to astrology, and is the author of two works on that science.

We hear of him again in 1620; for when the Privy Council in that year issued letters to all the nobility and gentry in England requesting a loan for the recovery of the Palatine, Sir Christopher, who earnestly solicited it, sent a letter to the Privy Council, informing them that the papists were as ready to assist the Emperor as the King was to assist the King of Bohemia. He informed them also that they met at the house of Sir Henry Kervile. He died at Baconsthorp in 1623, and is to be numbered among the benefactors of the Bodleian Library.*

For an account of the general style of this work, I must refer to the Introduction, for particular allusions, elucidation of words, etc., to the Notes. The poem is in the first place a satire, as Tourneur has condescended to inform us himself (see the fourth sonnet prefixed to it); it is a general description of the vices of the age (third sonnet), it is studiously written in such a way as to admit of general application only (fourth sonnet), and with the hope that it may rouse to action those who are either through sloth or bribery sunk in lethargy (third sonnet). The key to the poem is in English history at the time it appeared, *i.e.*, the dread

---

* See Blomefield's "Hist. of Norfolk," vol. vi., p. 507, and Wood's *Athen. Oxon.*, *sub* John Chamber.

and hatred of the Papal power, which was creating a great deal of alarm; the power of Spain, which was supported by Rome; the condition of Ireland, which Spain and Rome were endeavouring to incite against England; the expedition and death of Essex, and the consequent supposed depression of Art and Literature, of which he had ever been the ready and liberal patron; the hope that the coming King James VI. of Scotland would put everything right. It is entitled *The Transformed Metamorphosis* because, in the first part of the poem, he paints the world and the Church as metamorphosed by the causes stated above, from their normal and pristine state of purity and innocence: and, at the end of the poem, that same world and Church, as seen in the light of the new age, transformed back again. The work, I doubt not, was written partly to curry favour with the coming monarch, who could well understand and appreciate its grotesque and pedantic style, as well as to please Heydon, who was, very probably, a friend and partisan of James. If this view be the correct one, it is easy to understand the studied obscurity of its style, and the various "blinds" employed—such, for instance, as making the Unicorn feminine and the introduction of Queen Elizabeth, which perplex the course of the narrative. But the really obscure part of the poem lies really in these two questions: Who is meant by Mavortio? Who is the Unicorn " whose shining eyes of glorious eminence, doth all the world with brightness cleare adorn"? If these questions can be answered the enigma is solved.

Mavortio I take to be the Earl of Essex, and his exploits in the Delta to shadow his Irish expedition, for the following reasons:

1. The poem is dedicated to Sir Christopher Heydon, a keen and enthusiastic follower of Essex, who had served under him, who had been knighted by him, and who had imperilled his life by aiding in and abetting his rebellion.

2. Though the terms in which Essex is addressed in stanza 72 are almost identical with those in which Heydon is addressed in the prefatory sonnet, it would be preposterous to understand Mavortio as shadowing an obscure scholar like Heydon.

3. Stanzas 54 and 55 exactly describe the condition of Ireland before Spain and Rome began to tamper with it. See particularly Camden's "Hist. of Eliz.," folio, p. 617, while stanza 56 might well typify Clement VIII.'s attempts to win Ireland over to Spain. We know, for

instance, that in 1600 he sent to them a plenary Indulgence, and that in 1600 Spain, Ireland, and Rome were in league.

4. Stanzas 57 to 71 might well describe Essex's Irish campaign. That Tourneur should represent it as a success is not surprising, however inaccurate it may be. None of the Earl's panegyrists seem to have looked upon it as a failure, and in a black-letter ballad sung in the streets after his execution (preserved in the British Museum*) it would seem that it was popularly looked upon as a success.

5. Stanza 72 well applies to Essex, and may be compared with Spenser's eulogy in his "Prothalamion," line 145, and his sonnet to him. Stanza 73,

> "Of Heaven itself that but e'en now lamented
> The sun-fall of thyself," etc.

is an evident allusion to Essex's fall. So will all the following stanzas accurately apply to Essex. Stanza 79 is evidently a retrospection on Essex's exploit at Cadiz, and may be compared with Spenser's words:

> "Great England's glory and the world's wide wonder
> Whose dreadful name late through all Spain did thunder."

* See a "Lamentable Dittie on the Death of Robert Deverux." Black Letter. *Bagford Ballads,* vol. ii.

The stanza is characteristically obscure, and does not mean that he was *there* " when he on Thetis 'gan to thunder," etc., Delta's hope, but he is called Delta's hope because that title is associated with his name whether he is contemplated retrospectively or not. Again, in stanza 80,

> " When fatal Neptune with his trident keen
> Behind him hal'd him to his Thetisie,"

there is an allusion to his crossing St. George's Channel on his passage to England, and in the epithet *fatal* the poet probably alludes to the fact that it was Essex's precipitate departure from Ireland that ruined him, as was actually the case. To these arguments may be added the fact that Essex was looked upon as a bulwark of the Protestant religion—as the patron of art, as an accomplished poet, as a peerless soldier—as the probable saviour of Ireland: all which points are especially enlarged on in this poem. The objection that Essex was executed in 1601, and that this poem is dated 1600, will not go for much, for the chronology of these times is very loose. 1600 and 1601 might well be confounded, especially as Essex was executed at Easter. It is quite possible that as Tourneur was dealing with a nice question in a manner that might well have got him into the same difficulties as his patron, and increase his patron's difficulties too, he would supplement the studied obscurity of its style by mystifying the date.

That the Unicorn shadows James VI. of Scotland, who was looked upon as the heir to the English throne, and whose advent was even then hailed with impatient and ill-concealed joy by many, is probable, 1st, from the two marked allusions to the North in stanzas 89 and 94. "Her" I take to be a mere "blind," as also the allusion to Eliza (Elizabeth). The naked meaning of his lines would have cost the poet his head. 2nd. The Unicorn is represented as succeeding Mavortio. The people generally would have liked Essex to marry the Queen and to be their sovereign, mainly because of his staunch opposition to the Papists. He failing, they looked to James. 3rd. In stanza 91 there is an obvious allusion to James's patronage and love of learning.

The *probability* that Mavortio means Essex, Delta Ireland, and the Unicorn James VI., is strengthened moreover by the fact that most of the poem is obviously directed against the corrupt Papal Church, and the political mischief it was doing—that Essex was regarded as the protector of Protestantism, that the troubles in Ireland were regarded as being occasioned by Rome in her desire to help Spain ("Tyrone was in the pay of the King of Spain."—Camden. "The Pope likewise furnished him [Tyrone] with a large stock of indulgencies, besides mighty promises and a phœnix plume."—Id. page 617, folio edit.), and that James VI. was looked upon as the strenuous patron of Protestantism and opponent of Spain.

If these points are established, it will be easy to unravel the rest of the work.

The first six stanzas represent the poet as looking on a miserable and corrupted world—"a huge concavitie defect of light;" in the fourth stanza he identifies himself with that world which has been changed or metamorphosed from its pristine purity, fancifully comparing himself to the chaste Diana hearing of Lucretia's rape. Still, however, he can clearly discern a transformation imminent.

In stanza 7 he makes an appeal to the higher powers for assistance, and in stanzas 8, 9, 10, 11, 12 he describes how there is a general conspiracy against the Reformed Church on the part of the great powers, *i.e.*, Spain and the Papacy. But Heaven is asleep, and sees not the danger in which its earthly concerns are standing. Everything is corrupted and gone to perdition (st. 13). Where can the poet stand that he may clearly see the general misery? Is there no mead, or grove, or mountain? no! for the very mountains seek to obscure the sun; even that mountain which should be the world's admiration, Rome. The next three stanzas obviously describe the corrupt Church of Rome: he cannot take his stand there. In stanza 18 he abruptly appeals to the naval power of England, but at once checks himself, for no real help can come from that quarter. He is resolved, therefore, to take up an independent position, and to boldly confront and interpret the terrible state of things—" to be the chorus to the Tragedy." From stanza 23 to stanza 30 he describes the corruption of the Virgin Church, for particular references, allusions, etc., see the Notes. From stanza 31 to 36 he gives a fanciful picture of the Palace of Sin. In stanza 38 and 39 he alludes to a kind of folly lashed by Hall and Marston —avarice and foolish pride in a purchased pedigree. Stanzas 40 and 41 may allude to the Popes, usually old men, or to Whitgift. Stanza 42 is another appeal. From stanza 43 to 50 describes the metamorphosis of the Church from its virgin purity to pollution and corruption; for the particular allusions I refer to the Notes. In stanza 53 he passes on to another point—the political mischief which the corrupted Church was doing in Ireland, stanzas 54 and 55, both of which may be compared with Camden's remarks, "Never was Ireland stiller," etc.; see his Hist. under 1592. Stanzas 55 and 56 describe the machinations of the priests and emissaries sent over by the Pope to stir up Ireland against England, and to identify her with Spain. From stanza 57 to stanza 71 is an allegorical sketch of Essex's Irish campaign. The rest of the poem has been already dealt with.

THE PROLOGUE.

1

O Who perswades my willing errorie
  Into this blacke Cymerianized night?
  Who leades me into this concauitie,
This huge concauitie, defect of light,
  To feele the smart of Phlegetontike sight?
O who, I say, perswades mine infant eie,
To gaze vpon my youth's obscuritie?

2

What ashie ghost, what dead Cadaverie,
  What Geomanlike iaw howles in mine eares,
The ecchoized sounds of horrorie?
  What chaoized conciet doth forme my feares?
  What object is't that thus my quiet teares?
Who puts a flaming torch into my hand,
And bids me charily see where I stand?

3

Who fills my nosthrills with thicke foggy sents?
 Who feedes my taste with hony-smacking gall?
What pallid spirit tells of strange euents?
 Of euiternal night? of Phœbus' fall?
 Where is that Symphonie harmonicale,
Wherewith my heart was wont to tune sweet laies,
And teach my tongue to sing th' Æternall's praise?

4

O who, O who hath metamorphosed
 My sence? and plutoniz'd my heauenly shape?
What martyred Diana is't doth reade
 The tragicke story of Lucretia's rape?
 O who affrights me with blacke horrors gape?
Who tells me that the azure-colour'd skie,
Is now transform'd to hel's enuironrie?

5

Are not the lights that Jupiter appoynted
 To grace the heau'ns, and to direct the sight,
Still in that function which them first annoynted?
 Is not the world directed by their light?
 And is not rest the exercise of night?
Why is the skie so pitchie then at noone,
As though the day were gouern'd by the Moone?

Looke on my sight, you lycophosed eies,
    And tell me whether it be blear'd or no :
Daz'led with obiects contrarieties,
    With opposites of sad confused woe,
    Or els transpiercing ayre-cleare brightnes, loe
My eies, whether they be or dimm'd, or cleare,
Clearely discerne a Transformation neare.

THE TRANSFORMED METAMORPHOSIS.

WHENCE comes this? awake sad Mercurie
And Pegase-winged pace the milkie way:
Awake, heau'ns harbenger, awake and flie
To high Iehouah: O awake, I say,
Why sluggish Mercury, arte made of clay?
O where can life celestiall inherit,
If it remaines not in a heau'nly spirit?

Awake, O heau'n, for (loe) the heau'ns conspire;
The siluer feather'd Moone, and both the Beares,
Are poasted downe for Phlegetontike fire:
Loe, now they are vpon the azure spheares,
(Thy soule is vex'd with sense confounding feares)
Now are they mounted into Carol's waine,
With all the starres like to an armed traine.

I, euen those starres, which for their sacrad mindes
  (They once terrestriall) were stellified,
With all the force of Æol's saile—swell'd windes
  And fearefull thunder, vailer of earth's pride
  Vpon the loftie firmament do ride:
All with infernall concord do agree
To shake the strength of heauen's axeltree.

10

Eu'n from the artique to the antartique pole
  All in a rowe in ranke proportionate,
Subiect vnto th' vnstedfast moone's controle
  Do stand the lights that should truth animate
  And by their shine her woe extenuate.
With Phlegetonlike flame these tapers fed
Celestiall light haue quite extinguished.

11

O see how dampy shewes yond' torche's flame,
  Earth stop thy sent, for their infernall smell
  (O let me speake, lest I incurre heau'n's blame)
  With all thy arterizing strength expell,
  And make thy heart an agonizing hell.
See how their sulphur gathers to a cloud
And like blacke Orcus vault the earth doth shrowde.

12

What Morpheus rockes the sence of heau'n asleepe?
    Why heau'n awake: though long Endimionie
Hath pierc'd the clearenes of thy sight so deep,
    Thou can'st not see them prowdly mounted high;
    Yet maist thou heare them plot their treacherie.
Their treasons plotted, they with fiery shot,
Are driuing Phœbus from his chariot.

13

Loe, loe, the skie, whose hue was azurie,
    Is cloath'd with moorie Vesperugoe's coate,
The formed Chaos of this Cosmosie
    Is now transform'd to tawny Charon's boate;
    And on the Acheronticke maine doth floate.
Th' olimpique Globe is now a hollow ball
The huge concauitie blacke Plutoe's hall.

14

Where shall I stand, that I may freely view
    Earth's stage compleate with tragicke sceans of wo?
No meade, no grove, whose comfortizing hew
    Might make sad Terror my sad minde forgoe?
    No sun-grac'd mount soule-frighting horrors foe?
No sun-grac'd mount? how can the sun mounts grace
When mountaines seeke his count'nance to deface?

15

See, see, that mount that was the worlde's admire,
    The stately Pyramis of glorious price,
Whose seau'n hill'd head did ouer all aspire,
    Is now transform'd to Hydra-headed vice :
    Her hellish braine-pan of each enterprice.
On sinne's full number (loe) she is erect ;
For why ? Great Pluto was her Architect.

16

Blacke Auarice makes sale of Holines,
    And steeming luxurie doth broach her lust ;
Red-tyrannizing wrath doth soules oppresse,
    And cankred Enuie falsifies all trust,
    T' enrich her coffers with soule-choaking dust ;
On slowth and gluttonie they build their blisse,
Whereon they raise Ambition's Pyramis.

17

The frame's too slender for continuance,
    Too earthly high for soules to builde vpon ;
And of her strength my only esperance
    Is for to see her sad confusion ;
    Whose vapours are the worlde's infection.
Her high esteeme is of high heau'n despis'd ;
O see ere long her Babel Babelliz'd.

18

Where shall I finde a safe all-peacefull seat,
  To whose prospect the worlde's circumference
Presents it selfe? high Ioue I thee intreate
  Let Dodon's groue be lauish in expence,
  And scaffoldize her oakes for my defence.
Forgive me God, for help doth not consist
In Dodon's groue, nor a Dodonian fist.

19

Where shall I stand? O heau'n conduct me now;
  Ioue, Israellize my tongue, and let my voyce
Preuayle with thee; shew me the manner how
  To free me from this change: O soule rejoyce,
  For heau'n hath free'd me from black hel's annoies.
O see, O see, Ioue sets me free from thrall,
Such is his loue to them that on him call.

20

Loe, where I stand vpon a stedfast rocke,
  Whose peerlesse trust is free from all compare,
See how it brookes the Phlegetonticke shocke,
  And bides what foemen to each other share.
  The raging sea on this side doth it dare,
On that side flames; such is the earthly state
Of those from earth seeke them to alienate.

21

Now eies prepare, and be your sight as cleare
    As is the Skie, when none but Phaeton's sire
Inhabites it : for O (alas) I feare
    They will be dazled with smoake and fier,
    That with repulse of heau'n doth downe retire,
Heart, teach my tongue, directed by mine eie,
To be the Chorus to this tragedie.

22

Marke, you spectators of this tragicke act
    (If any rest vnmetamorphosed),
O you whose soules with hel are not contract,
    Whose sacred light is not extinguished;
    Whose intellectuall tapers are not fed
With Hell's flame : marke the transformation
Wrought by the charmes of this rebellion.

23

That sacred female which appear'd to him,
    Who was inspir'd with heau'ns intelligence,
Who was the last that drunke vpon the brim
    Of deepe diuining sacred influence :
    That heau'nly one, of glorious eminence;
She, whom Apollo clothed with his robe,
And plac'd hir feet vpon th' inconstant globe.

So cloath'd, his mantle might her shelter be,
  To shrowde her safe from Acheronticke mistes:
So plac'd, hir ground might feede hir egencie,
  Farre as it on necessitie consistes;
  And not t' exceede the bound of heau'nly listes
So cloath'd, she might to heau'n her minde applie:
So plac'd, to vse it in necessitie.

But (marke, O woe!) her high rebellious starres,
  (Their minds ambitioniz'd) do seeke her fall,
And hauing dim'd the Sun with smoaky warres,
  Haue found his dearest one how to appall;
  And mixe her honny with the bitterest gall.
See how her eies are fixed on the globe
Which, which, (O wo!) hath quite transform'd her robe.

Her robe, that like the Sun did clearly shine,
  Is now transform'd vnto an earthy coate
Of massive gold: because she did combine
  Affection with the Moon, and did remote
  Her heart from heau'n's book, where her name was
    wrote.
The globe takes head, that was her footstoole set:
And from her head doth pull her coronet.

Her twelve starred glorious coronet, (which Ioue
    Did make her temples' rich enuironrie,
And, for the more to manifest his loue,
    Encircled them with faire imbrodetie
    Of sacred lights in ayre-cleare azurie)
She is depriued off, and doth begin
To be the couerture of læthall sin.

28

The vine's Ædonides ; dead Murcianie ;
    Smooth Philoxenus ; murder's ground ;
Disquiet Eriphila ; hel's Syrenie ;
    Philocrematos ; the soule's deepe wound ;
    And whatso els in Hydra's head is found ;
Do maske themselues within her pleasing smile :
And so with deadly sinne the world beguile.

29

What dreadfull sight (O) do mine eies behold ?
    See, frosty age, that should direct aright
The grassie braine, (that is in vice so bold),
    With heedie doctrine and celestiall light ;
    Hath bin conuersing with hell's taper, night,
Whose diuelish charmes, like Circe's sorcerie,
Have metamorphosde Eos' Eonie.

30

Apolloe's herauld, that was wont to cheare
  Night-wounded soules with bright celest'all raies;
Faire Phosphorus (whose looke was wont to feare
  Infernall hagges, that haunt frequented wayes,
  To drawe the soule to hell that wand'ring strayes),
Is metamorphosde to a torch of hell;
And makes his mansion-house blacke horror's cell.

31

Whose deepe foundation's raisde from Phlegeton,
  The fi'rie riuer of blacke Orcus hall:
Whence pillers rise, which do themselues vpon
  Quadrangle wise, vphold Erebus wall:
  Worlde's trustlesse trust, soule's vnmistrusted fall.
Birds, vines, and flowres, and eu'ry sundry fruite
Do compasse it; for best that place they sute.

32

For since the spirit the bodie's pris'ner,
  Of heau'nly substance wholy is compact:
And since the flesh, the soule's imprisoner,
  Of excrementale earth is wholy fact:
  Since this with that itselfe cannot contract,
Needes must the soule (the earthly prison doubled
For all earth's pleasures' slime) be smothered.

33

From out the lake a bridge ascends thereto,
    Whereon in female shape a serpent stands,
Who eies her eie, or views her blew vain'd brow,
    With sence-bereauing gloses she inchaunts,
    And when she sees a worldling blind that haunts
The pleasure that doth seeme there to be found :
She soothes with Leucrocutanized sound.

34

Thence leades an entrie to a shining hal,
    Bedeckt with flowers of the fairest hew,
The Thrush, the Lark, and night's-ioy nightingale
    There minulize their pleasing laies anew,
    This welcome to the bitter bed of rue ;
This little roome will scarce two wights containe,
T' enioy their ioy, and there in pleasure raigne.

35

But next thereto adioynes a spacious roome,
    More fairely farre adorned than the other :
(O woe to him at sinne-awhaping doome,
    That to these shadowes hath his mind giu'n ouer),
    For (O) he neuer shall his soule recouer :
If this sweet sinne still feedes him with her smacke :
And his repentant hand him hales not backe.

36

The fraudfull floore of this deceitfull place
  Is all of quagmires, to entrap the wight
That treades thereon: yet couer'd o're with grasse
  Of youthfull hew, al pleasing to earth's sight.
  For so doth Satan worke his diu'lish spight.
This roome will centuries of worldes containe,
How small mirth's place, how large the place of paine.

37

Whoere's deceiu'd by this illusion,
  Must surely fall into this deepe abisse,
Downe to the horror of deepe Phlegeton,
  Whose fi'ry flames like vultures gnaw on flesh;
  Yet iote of it neuer consumed is.
O let no wight trust to this worldly sheene:
For such ioyes hate, of God, best loued beene.

38

Erinnis' purueyor, young elth I meane,
  Teares vp our mother's wombe to finde hir slime.
And doth ysearch her bowells all vncleane,
  For noysome filth; the poyson of our time,
  (Base dunghill slaue) for meanes for his to clime;
So may he well, for now earth's baddest good,
Makes eu'ry peasant seeme of gentle blood.

39

Yet certis, if the naked truth I say,
    Nor from the golden mine comes gentry true,
Nor can this age, the next, and so for ay
    Ech his succeeding age with it indue:
    For it's no heritage to heires t' ensue,
But shines in them to heau'n their minde that giue,
Then who doth so, in him doth gentrie liue.

40

O that old age (that kept the treasuries
    Of great Apollo once) whose falt'ring tongue
Intreates old earth performe his obsequies,
    Should now by hell be metamorphosde yong,
    And with desire of soule-infecting dong,
Seeke unto vice, weake infancie to winne,
And make his heart Epithesis of sinne.

41

The oldest man, saith ech day, one day more,
    One day? nay sure a twelve-months' time t'will be,
Ere seriant death will call me at my doore;
    Craz'd drooping age, why can thine eies not see
    Pale death arresting tender infancie?
O that his memory thee still would tell,
Now out of me might death my breath expell.

Where are the centinels? the armed watch,
   Who draw their breath from Phœbus' treasurie?
Somnus, awake; vnlocke the rustie latch,
   That leades into the caue's somniferie,
   Rowze vp the watch, lull'd with world's Syrenie,
Somnus, awake, pull off their golden maske,
And bid them strait finderesize their taske.

43

Somnus, awake: hell and the world conspire;
   Pan is transform'd, and al his flocke neere drown'd;
Pan that from heau'n receiu'd his due paid hyre,
   He that was wont, vpon the fertile ground
   Of Arcadie to feed, wherein was found,
No golden India that might preuent,
That high estate of poore, meane, rich content.

44

Pan, that was wont to make his *quiet life*,
   Th' exordium of ech soule-sweet argument;
Pan, that was wont to make his *voide of strife*,
   The period of ech sentence of Content;
   Temper'd with surrop of heau'n's document,
Pan, that was once a cleere Epitimie:
Is now transform'd to hot Epithymie.

O, where are they, Apollo did appoint,
    To guard Arcadia's sea-enuironed banckes?
The ocean's monarch, whom Ioue did annoint,
    The great controller of the whaly ranckes
    Is landed on Arcadia's tender flankes.
Enuie's protector, Pan, with gold hath fed:
And Pan with gold is metamorphosed.

46

Wealth's shipwracke; India's minerie;
    The pearly pibble which the Ocean keepes;
The Treasure-house of Neptune's Thetisie;
    The faire sweete poison of th' infernall deepes,
    Hell's twinckling instrument that neuer sleepes;
Is that great gift Tridentifer presents,
To make faire passage for his foule intents.

47

O see that head that once was couered
    With fleecy wooll, that hung on earth-low brakes,
Is scarce contented now, it selfe to wed,
    With what Eriphila from India takes,
    Now Pan of gold, himselfe a Cor'net makes.
His eies that 'fore were cleare lycophosie,
Now cannot see but in a minery.

48

His hand to pawes, his sheep-hooke to a mace,
  Are metamorphosed; his heart (whose height
Did ne're before o're-peere Arcadia's face)
  With cloud-high thoughts aspiring high is fraught,
  And chaoiz'd Ideas of conceit,
Doth make his gesture seem a troubled skie:
And fills his count'nance with sad meteorie.

49

Awake, O heau'n and all thy pow'rs awake,
  For Pan hath sold his flocke to Thetis' pheer:
O how the center of my soule doth quake,
  That barb'rous India should ouer-peer
  Fruiteful Arcadia, the world's great Peere!
Hot fiery dust, with trickling teares e'en weeps,
To see Arcadia's flockes drown'd in the deeps.

50

O how vnworthie's he a heard to be,
  That leaues his flocke for ech temptation!
As, into magistrates ech man may see,
  When by the means of vice th' are call'd vpon,
  To execute their duteous function;
O eu'n as they are knowne, when vap'rous vice,
Breathes forth a mist of blacke iniquities;

51

Eu'n so a shepheard tells where to hee's bent,
    When mighty Ioue after long summer's ioy,
(Of high celestiall kindnes to vs lent)
    Doth please vs trie with winter's sharp annoy;
    Or tempt his heart with earthly seeming ioy,
Which time, if he with care his flock doth feed,
Shewes loue to 's flock, and hate to 's earthly meed.

52

But though I speake 'gainst this hypocrisie,
    This hellish ill, o'remasked with holinesse,
Na'thlesse I neither can, nor wil deny,
    That if thereby we reaue no wight of blisse,
    We may preuent our earthly wretchednesse.
For lawfull 'tis our owne harme to preuent,
If not by ill we compasse our intent.

53

Is't possible the world should yet affoord,
    More cause of woe, then yet mine eies haue seene?
Can Pluto in his horror's cave yet hoord,
    More woe then in this tragicke sceane hath beene?
    Is't true I see? Or do I ouerweene?
O, O, I see more then I can expresse,
Amazed with sence-confounding wretchednesse.

54

In Delta that's enuiron'd with the sea,
    The hills and dales with heards are peopled,
That tend their tender flockes vpon the lea,
    And tune sweet laies vnto their pipes of reed,
    Meanewhile their flockes vpon the hillockes feed ;
And sometime nibble on the buskie root,
That did his tender bud but lately shoote.

55

Long while the heards enioy'd this sweet content,
    Not fearing wolues that might their flocks molest :
(For nothing harbor'd neare that harm them meant)
    And this content long might they have possest,
    Had not a beast spoil'd this their sweetned rest.
Whether the soile him bred, or foes him brought,
I doubt; seemes, some that Deltae's damage sought.

56

Among the shrubbes had set him priuily
    To spoyle the lambes that sometime did estray ;
Nor onely thus deuour'd them theeuishly,
    But oft allured them from out their way.
    With such chaung'd voice, no mortal wight could say
But that the notes were voice of man he sung :
O what deceit is lodged in the tongue ?

57

This dayly spoyle through ech man's eare did runne,
    At length Mavortio, a gallant Knight,
The meane whereby his Country honor wonne,
    Heard of the harme wrought by Hyenna's spight:
    Scarce heard he of the spoyle, but that his sp'rite
Æthereall (not hable to endure
His heart should knowledge of such harme immure

58

An houre, and th' wrong rest vnirrooted out)
    Him draue, as sail-swel'd barks are droue by wind,
And strait he arm'd him (mounting 's prancer stout);
    He forward pricks, spurr'd by a noble mind,
    Awaited on by Truth, his Page, full kind,
And by a 'squire that artfull strength was call'd:
Seem'd, Hercules him could not haue appall'd:

59

Thus (pricking on the plaine) at last he ey'd
    The grisly beast as in her den she lay,
Tearing a lamb with iawes farre stretch'd awide,
    A seely lambkin which she made her pray,
    Straight with a courage bold began assay
How he could buckle with the monsters force:
Not meaning once to harbor mild remorce.

Downe he alighted from his milk-white steed,
  And gaue him Veramount to walk o' th' plaine ;
Then stept to th' monster with a wise-bold heed,
  Thou monstrous fiend (quoth he) thy pray refrain,
  For with my sword Ile work thy mortall paine :
The beast gan looke as one that were adrad,
Fearing her future hap would proue full bad.

At length, as one that from a traunce awakes,
  She stretched foorth her self vpon the ground ;
And to her cursed tongue herselfe betakes,
  Hoping hir speech wold yield best aid that stound.
  Faire Sir, (quoth she) t'is said this soile hath found,
That I have brought this Countries good to spoyle :
But (Knight) belieue me, I have t'ane much toile.

To feare the wolues with changed voyce of tong,
  When they have e'en beene ready to assaile
The ewes that haue beene suckling their yong :
  Then hath my speech their purpose causde to faile :
  My very heart doth bleede ; O how I waile
To thinke vpon the spoyle the wolues would make ;
Did not my Care them force their prey forsake ?

63

To her Syrenian song, the Knight gaue eare,
  And noted in her speech how subtill Arte,
Her gesture framde to eu'ry word so neare,
  That (had he beene a man of massiue hart)
  He would haue melted at her Mermaide's part:
But he being a Knight of noble spirit:
Her tongue could not him of his heart dis'nherit.

64

But spurr'd him to reuenge the spoyle she made;
  (Commixt with poyson of hypocrisie)
He strait vnsheathes his trusty steeled blade,
  And (silent) doth demonstrate presently,
  The bottome of his mind effectually.
Soone as she feeles the smart, she startes abacke,
And (for defence) with poyson hellie blacke

65

For hurled from her wide stretcht foaming throat,
  She thinkes t' infect the vninfected Knight:
But stowt Mauortio wore a steeled coate,
  So iunctly ioynted, that in all their sight,
  Her hellish poyson neuer enter might;
(All were it natur'd still to search for way:)
To saue hir life by hir foes' liue's decay.

66

Short had the fight bin, had she only beene,
  (And great his honour by hir only death)
But eu'ry drop of bloud his sword all keene,
  Causde issue from hir noysome steeming breath,
  Transformed were to monsters on the heath.
All with their poyson like a rounding ring:
The good encombred Knight encompassing.

67

So that the more that she entroped him,
  (By deadly gaspes) the conquest soone would end;
The more his labour sprung: and seem'd to dim
  Eftsomes (alas) the hope his toile did send.
  Yet he of all was victor in the end.
And for this act vntill the end his fame,
Will through the world high raise Mavortio's name.

68

The Knight (about to sheathe) chanc'd turne his eie,
  And spies the multitude that him enround:
Nay (then quoth he) no time approacheth nie,
  To take our leaues of this thiefe-harb'ring ground
  Before Apollo Thetis lap hath found,
They all shall die; if heau'n doth smiling stand:
Viewing the heart of his Mavortio's hand.

69

His 'squire with artfull courage aides his Knight:
  Both vsde their blades vnto so good auaile,
That who had ei'd this bloudy fi'rie fight,
    Might here see maimed wights low creeping traile
    Their owne hew'd limbes, there gasping iawes that waile
To see their limbs lopt from their bodies lie,
On hugie heapes, like vnto mountaines high.

70

And twixt the streams of steaming blod swift running
  With bloudles trunks, lop'd heads, legs, thighs and armes,
Vpon the riuer like dead fishes swimming;
    Ere Sol with Neptune sleeped, slept their harmes;
    All being shooke with death's all deadly charmes.
O happy houre! that so Mavortio ioy'd:
To see the monsters by his arme destroy'd.

71

This noble conquest made him famoized,
  By all the heards throughout the Deltan soile,
Who vow'd his name should be aeternized,
    (Despight of Fortune and her trustlesse foyle)
    In memorizing lines, which worldly broyle,
Nor Enuie's canker, neuer should deface,
Long as the world retaines her worldly face.

O peerelesse worth! O worth Mavortian!
    Heau'n vpholding Atlas; warre's melodie;
Knight of the lilly; heauen's champion;
    Arte's patron; Muses' dearest Adonie;
    Vrania's soule refreshing Castalie;
Worthy the world; the world not worthy thee:
That art deem'd worthy of the deitie.

3

Of heauen it selfe, that but eu'n now lamented
    The sun-fall of thy selfe, whom heau'n (disdained)
Whom heau'n's high trinaty was not contented,
    That in the world thy spirit be contained,
    But there shuld dwel where Ioue himself remained;
For that on earth thy spirit earth directed,
Heau'n hath thy spirit for high heau'n elected.

4

While heau'n did daigne the world should him inioy,
    The ninefold Sorory themselues exiled,
Euen from their natiue home to art's annoy,
    From twin-topt mount, vnto a place defiled,
    (Where pined writ and starved art compiled)
Their harm they knew, and harm with heart imbraced,
To nurse their deare heart by their cheap art graced.

75

  Graced by nurses (art's nurse highly grac'd him)
     Who fed him with pure marrow of the Muses;
  And when he list, with moisture to refresh him,
     He drunke cleare Helicon: cleare from abuses,
     He bent his mind to pure Vranian vses,
Vranianie him did to heau'n vpreare:
And made to man, him demi-god appeare.

76

  Since wisedome then vpreares a man to heau'n,
     Since wisedome then (that doth high God adore)
  When he of all that earth yeelds is bereau'n,
     When all els failes, doth God-like him decore,
     O world erect thy blisse on wisedome's lore.
The greatest man decores not wisedome's horne:
But wisedome doth the meanest wight adorne.

77

  Pieria's darling; cleare-streaming Helicon;
     Bœotia's pearle; the nine voic'd harmony;
  Heart crystalline; tongue pure Castalion;
     Delta's Adamant; Elizium's melody;
     Vrania's selfe, that sung coelestially;
Was then for Mars apt, by the Muses nurs'd,
For Mars his knights, are 'squires to th' muses first.

78

Downe to the world descended Mars at length,
    When the Pierides had knit the veines,
That from his heart did giue his body strength
    With soule-sweet Manna, marrow of the reines ;
    Downe he descended, and no whit disdaines
To liue on earth, leauing the sacred skies
Only the muses deare to Martialize.

79

But (O) when Delta's hope, the muses' wonder,
    Foe's feare, feare's foe, Ioue's martialist,
On Thetis gan like to a fearefull thunder
    Make Hydra shake with a Dodonian fist;
    When Delta deem'd her selfe in him thus blest,
Then Delta of her hope was quite bereaued ;
See how the world is by the world deceiued !

80

The Phœbus of his soile, scarce shew'd his sheen,
    And fac'd the West with smiling Aurory,
When fatall Neptune with his trident keene,
    (Behind him) hal'd him to his Thetisie,
    But Ioue downe sent swift-winged Mercurie,
And charged him to lay him 's wings vpon,
And be the conuoy of his champion.

81

When Mercurie approch'd the seat of Ioue,
 With Mavors spirit on his winged arme;
Ioue daign'd descend downe from his seat aboue,
 And him imbraced with all heau'nly charme.
 Aboue the lofty skies, deuoid of harme
Sits Mavors spirit, as a demi-god:
Instead of Mars, swaying his warlike rod.

82

While Mars himselfe goes wandring vp and downe,
 Associated with the sacred brood,
That hand in hand (like an enchaining rowne)
 Encompasse him: eu'n dead with want of food
 If want may heau'n hurt with deadly bood)
Much teen they bide in search for such an one:
Whom they may make their nurs'rie's paragon.

83

A pitchie night encurtained with clowdes
 (That kept from it heau'n's star-bright comforture
Is the sole Theater that them enshrowdes;
 Fogs, damps, trees, stones, their sole encompassure,
 To whom they mone, black todes giue responsure;
Their woe is like vnto that wretches paine,
Whom ('s parents dead) no man will entertaine.

84

Before that death by life had stellified
    Great Mavors spirit in the loftie skie:
Before his spirit in heau'n was deified,
    Mars and the Muses had their dignity,
    The sacred sisters did him aptifie
For Mars: he kindly fed his parents' want,
And made that plenty which before was scant.

85

But now (O woe) they long may go vnfed.
    Ayde (mighty Ioue) for Nilus' Crocodiles
Are battring in the pure Castalian head.
    Pure horse-foot Helicon, their filth defiles,
    Art, like Ægyptian dogs, must scape their wiles.
O dreary woe! the Muses did but sup,
And are infected with that pois'nous cup.

86

How like blacke Orcus lookes this dampy caue,
    This obscure dungeon of Cimmerian sin,
This hugy hell! my spirit gins to raue,
    To see blacke Pluto banquetting within
    The once-form'd world with his faire Proserpin.
O see the world, all is by heau'n reiected,
Now that the sacred Muses are infected.

87

See, where Vrania, onelie's seated on
   The twin-top'd hill, the steepie craggy mount,
That ouer-peeres, (once) cristall Helicon:
   There bides she eu'ry storme, that once was wont
   To bathe her selfe in the Castalian fount.
Yet this me gladdes, though she of ioy be reau'n,
Yet is she now come neerer vnto heau'n.

88

O where's Mavortio? may the Muses say:
   And haue the heau'ns bereaued vs of blisse?
O heau'ns! nay O sweet heau'n-fed Muses stay.
   Exclaime not on the sacred heau'ns for this:
   But as a mother (that her childe doth misse)
Lament: and be your heart from despaire wonne:
Your wombe may bring forth such another sonne.

89

And as thy sunne not still could face the north,
   But by his falling reaued thee of day;
(Because the day light's by the night put forth)
   Nor can thy night's blacke hew endure alway:
   Then hope sweet Delta hope, from murmure stay,
Thy Phœbus slumbreth but in Thetis' lap:
Hee'l rise before thou thinkst of such a hap.

90

See that same rocke, the rocke of my defence,
  Is metamorphosde to an Vnicorne:
Whose shining eies of glorious eminence,
  Doth all the world with brightnes cleare adorne,
  And with Ioue's strength, hir life-preserving horne,
Hath purified the cristallized fount,
That streames along the valley of Artes' mount.

91

Her streaming rayes haue pierc'd the cloudie skies,
  And made heau'ns traitors blush to see their shame;
Cleared the world of her black vironries,
  And with pale feare doth all their treason tame.
  Delta's Bellonian, (name of peerelesse fame)
Hath free'd Apollo from their treacherie,
And plac'd him in his former dignitie.

92

Come, come, you wights that are transformed quite,
  Eliza will you retransforme againe;
Come star-crown'd female and receiue thy sight,
  Let all the world wash in her boundlesse maine,
  And for their paine receiue a double gaine.
My very soule with heau'nly pleasure's fed,
To see th' transform'd metamorphosed.

Vrania sits amid Pernassus vale,
    O're shelterd with an aire-cleare Canopie:
  O sense's nurse! soule-sweet refreshing dale,
    God's nectar; heau'n's sweet ambrosianie;
    Conuert each riuer to pure Castalie.
That India it selfe, may sweetly raise,
Her well tun'd notes in high Iehouah's praise.

THE EPILOGUE.

NOW are the pitchie Curtains (that enclosde
    The heau'nly radiance of Apollo's shine)
    Drawne backe: and all that in hel's caue reposd
Are dauncing chearely in a siluer twine,
    With heau'n's Vrania, shaming Proserpine.
Hell's Phlegetontike torches are put forth:
And now the Sunne doth face the frosty north.

Sacred Apollo cheeres the lightsome day,
    And swan-plum'd Phœbe gards the star-faire night,
Lest Pluto's forester, should cause estray,
    Darke Cosmo's Pilgrims wandring without light;
    Heau'n's sacred lights agree in one consent,
Heau'n's sacred lights agree in one consent,
To drive the clowdes from foorth the firmament.

THE EPILOGUE.

    Now is the Moone not blemisht with a cloud,
        Nor any lampe (that should illuminate
    And lighten eu'ry thing that heau'n doth shrowd)
        Darkned; or else my sight gin's to abate,
        And 's reaued of it's intellectuate.
Each obscure caue is lightned by the day:
Or else mine eyes are forced to estray.

    But when my heart was vrged fourth to breath,
        Fell accents of soule-terrifying paine;
    My subject was a heau'nly taper's death;
        Night was my lampe; my inke, hel's pitchy maine:
        Then blame me not, if my wittes light did waine,
Since but with night I could with none conferre
In this my Epinyctall register.

FINIS.

NOTES TO THE TRANSFORMED METAMORPHOSIS.

Errorie. That is, state of wandering. In the original and Latin sense of the word: "Who persuades me to wander willingly into," etc. We may mention once for all that the termination "ie" in this poem—when it is appended to words not naturally ending in "y"—usually has the force of "a state or condition of." Cf. "horrorie;" Endimionie being in the state of Endymion, in a state of sleep; Murcianie, in a state of sloth; "eonie," "azurie," "somniferie." It is merely an abused and perverted extension of the Latin "ia," as in *prudentia, infantia,* etc., and our "cy" as in "infancy." In the word "sororie" it would seem to = hood, sisterhood.

Cymerianized. A night made like that of the Cimmerii. The epithet Cimmerian is common enough in our classics, even as late as Campbell, who speaks in his *Pleasures of Hope* of

"Cimmerian darkness in the parting soul."

Phlegetontike. A word which seems to have had a great charm for Tourneur, is, of course, by metonymy for hellish.

To gaze upon, etc. To gaze upon that which is darkening or obscuring my youth.

Cadaverie = Cadaver = corpse.

Geomantike. This word is an adjective formed indirectly from the Greek, and directly from the Italian *geomante,* explained by Florio to be a "sorcerer that works by circles or pricks on the earth," or *geomontia,* the art of enchanting by circles or pricks in the earth. It means here, then, "What sorcerer's jaw," or "What sorcerer is howling in my ears," etc.

Ecchoized. This barbarous word simply = echoed.

Chaoized conceit. What confused image, or imagination.

Charily = Cautiously, as often.

Eviternal. The uncontracted form of eternal.

Plutonized = Made like Pluto; made my heavenly shape a hellish shape.

Lycophosed. Cf. *infra,* "His eyes that 'fore were pure lycophosie." This is a good instance of Tourneur's Alexandrianism. The word means "sun-clear," or made like the sun. λυκόφως, from which it is immediately taken, signifies twilight, or, as the old commentators, who derived it from λύκος, a wolf, explain, the time when wolves prowl. But in a curious passage in Macrobius's *Saturnalia,* lib. i. cap. 17, we learn that the sun was worshipped under the name of a wolf, and that the word λύκος was synonymous with sol, or, in other words, with light. "λύκον autem *solem* vocari etiam Lycopolitana Thebaidos civitas testimonio est quæ pari relligione *Apollinem* itemque *lupum* hoc est λύκον colit, in utroque solem venerans."

With objects' contrarietie, etc. An image probably suggested by the logical square of opposition. This appears to mean, "Lo, my eyes, whether they be dazzled with all the woes that confront them and so are dimmed, or whether they pierce into clear pure air, and so are clear, still, however that may be, they discern a transformation."

Mercurie—Jehovah. All through the poem he confuses as grotesquely as Sannazarius and Vida the classical with the Christian mythology.

Awake, O heaven, etc. The best commentary on these two stanzas, which I shall not make myself ridiculous by attempting to explain, is a similarly portentous passage in Dryden's *Annus Mirabilis*:

"Then we upon our orb's last verge shall go
 And see the ocean leaning on the sky,
From thence our rolling neighbours we shall know,
 And on the lunar world securely pry."

The unsteadfast man's control. He is now, I presume, beginning to touch on the corruption of the foremost men in the Church. It may be over-subtle to suspect there is an allusion to Innocent III.'s famous and favourite image of the secular power being the moon, the lesser light—as the spiritual power is the sun, the greater light. Innocent vested both these powers in the Church; Tourneur may have separated the powers, but preserved the image. We may then interpret, "The lights that should animate truth have sold themselves to forward the interest of the secular power," as Clement VIII. actually did assist Spain.

With—arterizing. The printed copy reads *with*, which I have altered into *will*. The monstrous word arterizing I interpret thus: It is taken from the Italian *arteggiare*, which Florio explains as "to artize, to live by an art, to show art or skill." Tourneur adds the syllable "er" to suit the purposes of his verse, and so it will mean, "With all the art, or skill, or the strength possessed by you can apply."

Orcus. Hell.

Endimonie. State of Endymion; state of sleep; lethargy.

Vesperugoe is the evening star; cf. Plautus, *Amphitruo*, i. i. 119:
 "Nec Jugulæ, neque Vesperugo neque Vergiliæ recidunt."

The formed chaos, etc. An awkward oxymoron. The general meaning is that the whole universe has gone—in cœlum.

Mounts grace. *I.e.*, grace mountains.

Brain-pan. *I.e.*, skull; so the head which frames or devises. Cf. *Henry VI. Part II.* iv. 10: "Many a time but for a sallet my *brain-pan* had been cleft with a brown-bill."

Sins full number. Seven deadly sins. An ingenious allusion to her Seven Hills.

Luxurie. See note on act i. sc. 1. of the *Revenger's Tragedy*.

Esperance, etc. A French word which has held its own. Cf. *Lear*, iv. i. etc.:

"Stands still in *esperance*, lives not in fear."

Babel babellized. Her impious Babel coming to the fate of Babel.

Let Dodon's grove. It would seem that he is making a desperate appeal to the naval power of England to put things right. The oak-groves of Dodona were of course very celebrated. Howel wrote a work called *Dodona's Grove*. The verses which preface it may serve to illustrate Tourneur's reference:

"From the pure air of Greece, th' ancient source
Of Learning, and Philosophie's chief source,
Dodona sends her trees to re-salute
The Queen of Isles."

See also Hall, book iii. sat. 1.

Dodonian fist. Is Tournerian for any *assistance* which can come from Dodona? Fist = hand = arm = physical help.

Of those, etc. Of those who seek to estrange themselves from the world.

That sacred female, etc.

An allusion to *Revelation* xii. 1. "And there appeared a great wonder in heaven, a woman clothed with the sun, and the moon under her feet, and upon her head a crown of twelve stars."

And having dimmed the sun, etc.

Cf. *Revelation* ix. 2 : " And there arose a smoke out of the pit as the smoke of a great furnace, and the sun and the air were darkened by reason of the smoke," etc. For these references to the *Apocalypse* I am indebted to the kindness of the Rev. A. B. Grosart.

And mix her honey, etc.

Cf. before "Feeds my taste with honey smacking gall."

Affection with the moon, etc.

Cf. former note on stanza 10.

Remote her heart, etc.

What barbarous precedent he may have for turning a past participle into a transitive verb, I know not.

Her twelve starred, etc.

Cf. Revelations xii. 1.

Embrodelie. Embroidery, a not uncommon form of the word.

The Vines, Ædonides, etc.

The general meaning of this stanza is *drunkenness—sloth, gluttony,* murderous hypocrisy, strife and *avarice* are latent in her fair exterior. He condenses the vices typified by certain mythological or historical personages and the vices denoted by the derivation of their names. Thus, Ædonides = drunkenness, for the Edonides (as the word should rather be spelt) were the priestesses of Bacchus, so called because they celebrated their rites on Mount Edon. See the commentators on Ovid, *Met.* ii. 65.

Murcianie = Sloth, for Murcia was apparently the Goddess of Sloth ; see Drakenborch on Livy, lib. i. cap. 33 : " *Murcia* quasi *Murtea.* Murtea autem primo dicta fuerat vel quia myrtus Veneri sacra, vel a Myrteto," etc. "*Alii Murciam desidiæ deam fuisse quæ homines murcidos sive ignavos faceret.* The word means here then sloth, a state of sloth, the termination "ie" being added, as in "Endemonie," etc., and the *n* inserted for the sake of euphony.

Smooth—Philoxenus. Gluttony and murderous hypocrisy. "The smyler with the knyf under his cloke"—Philoxenus was a notorious glutton. "Φιλοξένος λίχνος ἦν καὶ γαστερος ἥττων," as Ælian, *Var. Hist.,* x. 9, informs in a chapter which tells rather a pointless anecdote about him. See plenty on the interesting individual in *Athenæus,* lib. i. 8, 9, 10. He is said to have wished to have the neck of a crane that the pleasures of the palate might be prolonged.

Murder's ground. He now deals with the vice suggested by the name φιλόξενος, or hospitable, and calls him the ground on which murder bases its accents, or its tune, ground being an old musical term : *i.e.*, the smooth-toned pipe on which murder plays; in other words, he pretends hospitality that he may work his murderous purpose.

Disquiet Eriphila. Another false quantity=personified avarice, as in stanza 47, "with what Eriphila from India takes," an allusion of course to Eriphyle, the wife of Amphiaraus, who betrayed her husband for a golden necklace; also personification of Strife or Discord, from φιλὸς and ἔρις, φιλὴ ἐριδὺς. Tourneur has amply proved himself capable of playing this trick with the genitive case, and transposing the words.

Philocrematos. Avarice, a name coined simply from the derivation φιλεῖν and χρῆμα, φιλὸς and χρήματος.

Grassie. Probably from the Italian *grasso,* expl. Florio, fat, rich, fertile.

Frostie age. If there is any particular allusion here it may refer to Bancroft, who in 1597 was made Bishop of London, and was virtually Archbishop of Canterbury, as Whitgift, now old and infirm, entrusted everything to him. Bancroft was excessively unpopular with the poets of the age, and was *popularly suspected* of *abetting and favouring the Papists*. See particularly Sir John Harrington's *Brief View of the Church, etc.*, where he defends Bancroft against the charge of papacy, etc.

Eos, Eonie. Have changed or metamorphosed morning, etc. Properly *Eos*, state of being *Eos*, or morning.

To fear. I.e., to scare or terrify. Cf. *Measure for Measure*, act ii. sc. 1.:

"Setting it up to *fear* the birds of prey."

Whose deep foundations, etc.

For the general meaning of the following stanzas see Introduction.

Who ever her eie, etc.

I.e., She stands there and with flatteries that bereave him of his senses enchants everyone who meets her eye or gazes on her brow.

Leucrocutanized sound.

This monstrous word may be explained, I think, in two ways; of the first interpretation I am doubtful, of the second tolerably confident.

1. With a voice or with accents whetted by the thought of gain to be obtained from getting the worldling into her power; from *lucrum* and *acutus*, or rather *acutare*, a barbarous word for which *vid. Du Cange* Glossary. Tourneur would be quite capable of giving *acutus* the force of a past participle from *acutare*. A man who could write Erēbus, with the "e" long, see stanza 31, would be equal to anything.

2. With the strains of a *Leucrocuta*, which we will leave honest Florio to describe. "A beast that hath all his teeth of one piece, as big as an ass, with neck, tail, and breast like a lion, and a head like a camel, and counterfeits the voice of a man." See art. Leucrocuta in his *World of Words*. She soothes, that is to say, with a strain which is the voice of a foul and frightful monster.

Minulize. Probably for minurize, which is taken directly from the Greek μινυρίζειν to sing or warble, through the Latin *minurire*, which means the same.

Sin-awhaping. Sin-confounding. To awhape is to terrify or confound. Cf. Chaucer: *passim.*

And Spenser:
"Deeply do your sad words my wits *awhape*,"
quoted by Nares.

Eeth. For eald—young age, so youth; though the word is used occasionally for youth. Cf. *Fairfax' Tasso:*
"For the guard
Of noble Raimond from his tender eild."

Epithesis of sin. This is a sense of the Greek word ἐπίθεσις, common in theology of St. Paul, *Epist. to Timothy*, i. 4. 14, *Irenæus*, etc., and is the word used for "confirmation" or the laying on of hands; so here it means, his heart a subject for Sin to lay its hands on; or, in other words, for sin to confirm.

Ere serjeant death. Cf. *Hamlet*, act v. sc. 2.
"As this fell serjeant death
Is strict in his arrest."

Sinderesize. This hideous word is taken from the Greek συντήρησις through the Latin *synteresis*, which latter word is explained by Minsheu as meaning "the pure part of conscience." Minsheu changes, like Tourneur, the "t" into "d" and spells the substantive *sinderesi*. The word *synderesis* occurs twice in Marston:

"So cold and dead is his *synderesis.*"
Scourge of Villainy, sat. xi., and:
"Return, return sacred synderesis."
Id., sat viii. It means here, then, bid them purify or make conscientious their task.

Pan that was won't, etc. All that follows about Pan, which typifies the pure, uncorrupted Church, is modelled closely on Spenser. See particularly Shepherd's Calender, *May*, *July*, and *September*, passim.

Clear epitimie, hot epithemie.

These two words are to be explained according to their proper meaning in the Greek, from which they are immediately taken, ἐπιτίμια and ἐπιθυμία.

Pan that was once noble ambition personified, is now mere lust and greed personified.

Envie's Protector. He who is the supported or protector of Envy has fed Pan with gold.

Minerie. This is direct from the Italian *minera*, which means "a mine that yields metals," Florio—so here, wealth.

Is that great gift, etc.

Cf. Introduction.

Eriphila. See note on stanza 28.

Lycophosie. See note on former stanza.

But in a minerie.

Cannot see but in a mine, cannot see but when it is in the midst of gold.

Meteorie. Direct from the Italian *meteore*, meaning meteors.

Hath sold his flock, etc.

See Introduction.

Pheere—for pheere, pheare, or fere, which here means husband, and alludes to the King of Spain. See Nares' excellent article.

Adrad. Frightened or terrified.

Poison hellic black, etc.

This description was probably suggested by Spenser's description of the fight between the Errour and the Red-Cross Knight. *Faery Queen*, i. 1.

Heart of his hand.

With this ludicrous image may be compared a verse quoted by Coleridge in his *Biographia Litteraria* :

"Or round my *heart's leg* tie his galling chain."

Should be eternized. Cf. Lodge *Fig for Momus,* ecl. 3 : "Let thy fame *eternize* thy deserts."

The nine-fold sororie. Sisterhood : the Muses.

He drunk pure Helicon. Essex was a poet.

Delta's adamant. Magnet. Cf. Webster *Vitt. Corom.*: "You are the adamant shall draw her to you."

A Dodonia fist.

Cf. note on stanza 10.

Down to the world.

Essex is here identified with Mars, and is represented as leaving heaven on the completion of his education by the Pierides, to live on earth, leaving no one to represent him in heaven except the loved Muses, of whom he was a votary.

Hal'd him to his Thelesie, etc.

See Introduction.

Much teen they bide. Sorrow. Cf. *Rich. III.*, act. iv. sc. 1. : "Each hour's joy wreck'd with a week of *teen*."

Art like Egyptian dogs, etc.

This is an allusion to a curious anecdote in Ælian, *Var. Hist.* i. 4, where he says that the dogs on the banks of the Nile, owing to their terror of the crocodiles in the river, only drink by snatches, and cannot quench their thirst.

Epinyctal register. Nocturnal. From the Greek ἐπυνυκτίς, which means a night-book.

THE END.

www.ingramcontent.com/pod-product-compliance
Lightning Source LLC
Chambersburg PA
CBHW021824230426
43669CB00008B/860